W I

RISE OF A
LIGHTWORKER

The unfolding true story of journeys into the spirit realm

Copyright © 2018 by Will Sibley.

All rights reserved. No part of this book may be reproduced or transmitted in any form or by any means, electronic or mechanical, including photocopying or recording without the permission of the author. All rights reserved.

Proofediting by Earl Colwell

Cover and layout by www.spiffingcovers.com

Preface

I felt inspired to write this book, as an account of true and factual experiences from my life, which led me ultimately on an incredible spiritual adventure.

I want to share the personal discoveries I have made that demonstrate evidence that we are not alone, that we are all multidimensional, eternal beings with the ability to connect with our deceased loved ones' as well as other entities that seek to assist mankind.

Everything happens for a reason, there are no chance events. If you are drawn to read this book, I hope it offers encouragement, enlightenment and reassurance to other *lightworker's* who find themselves on a similar journey.

There are many different definitions for describing a *lightworker*. For me it is somebody that has grown up feeling an inner sense that they have a purpose greater than just existing or operating in everyday life. Often these people have gone through adversity and hit rock bottom, before discovering there is more to life than just material gains and losses. They have an empathy with others' and an affinity with nature that enables them to connect with people at a deeply sensitive and emotional level. They see an inner beauty in everyone no matter what their background is. They may discover they have a particular skill in teaching, or they may even have amazing abilities such as mediumship or healing.

Death is nothing at all. It does not count.

I have only slipped away into the next room. Nothing has happened.

I am I, and you are you, and the old life that we lived so fondly together is untouched, unchanged.

Whatever we were to each other, that we are still. Call me by the old familiar name. Speak of me in the easy way you always used. Put no difference into your tone. Wear no forced air of solemnity or sorrow.

Laugh as we always laughed at the little jokes we always enjoyed together.

Play, smile, think of me, pray for me.

Let my name be ever the household word that it always was. Let it be spoken without effort, without the ghost of a shadow in it. Life means all that it ever meant. It is the same as it ever was.

There is absolute unbroken continuity.

What is death but a negligible accident?

Why should I be out of mind because I am out of sight?

I am waiting for you for an interval, somewhere very near, just around the corner. All is well. Nothing is hurt, nothing is lost. One brief moment and all will be as it was before. How we shall laugh at the trouble of parting when we meet again !

Henry Scott Holland (1847-1918)
Canon of St. Paul's Cathedral

My sincere gratitude goes out to Debbie for her dedication to my spiritual development and to Jacquie and Karen for the powerful circle we created together.

To Jules, for her support and inspiration.

To my parents Colin and Gwen and my Spirit guides for all their direction and assistance on this incredible Spiritual journey of discovery.

I dedicate this book to my three children Ashleigh, Luke and Kane.

Contents

1. My story 11
2. Awakening 55
3. Connection with Spirit 77
4. Healing experiences 88
5. Developing with Spirit 128
6. Multi-dimensional work 138
7. Raising our vibration 148
8. The End Game 156

My story

I have always said that if I were to ever write an autobiography it would be entitled "William-Bill-Will ", and the reason for this is that I can now, with the knowledge and experience I have gained, reflect and retrospectively appreciate, that there were very distinct periods in my life where I interacted in a different way with family, friends and the community. I believe you can experience or witness something; a behaviour, an interaction or an encounter of some kind, at an early age, which will potentially shape your development as a personality, and that this can either have a positive or negative influence upon you.

I was born August 27, 1967 William Edward Arthur Want-Sibley, at Chase Farm Hospital, North London, the first child of my parents Colin Want-Sibley and Gwyneth Louise Want-Sibley.

Two years later my brother James Adrian George was born, our father named us after the kings of England, which was fine if you lived in a posh area like Hampstead, but not so cool when you lived in Barrow Close, Winchmore Hill. To make matters worse, Barrow Close was a cul-de-sac of about a hundred houses, the first six houses were privately owned and the rest were Church Army subsidised rental homes. The owners' of the first six houses applied to the council to get a street name of their own so they weren't associated with the Church Army properties .

Therefore the street sign at the start of our street said (Temple Gardens leading to Barrow Close) and we lived at number 3 Temple Gardens. This was just pure snobbery in my view and alienated our family somewhat from the rest of the street.

My early years were quite settled. I attended Winchmore Hill Primary School, a three story Victorian building, and pretty much cruised through that lacklustre education, not really taking much in, which led to my form teacher discovering, when I was aged nine that I could hardly read and had been copying other students' work.

As a result, I was then sent to a special needs class for children with learning difficulties, located in the attic room of the school and accessed by a frighteningly narrow staircase high above the main spiral stairwell, where we had to queue during class change over, which I hated because all the other pupils would walk past us and sneer at us. This made me knuckle down in earnest so that I could get back to the main English class.

By the time I was due to apply and enrol in secondary school aged eleven, I wasn't really best prepared in terms of academic capabilities. My parents and I were summoned to a meeting with the headmaster, who was of the opinion that I should stay on at Junior school for another year. I recall begging, crying and pleading with them to let me go to secondary school where all my friends were going and eventually they gave in and I was given a place at Winchmore Senior School, which was literally and directly across the other side of the road from my Primary School.

Day one of secondary school had a profound effect on me I have to say. All new pupils were required to be herded into a large sports hall/makeshift assembly hall, not many knew each other. We all sat cross legged, waiting for our respective form teachers', who all stood in a parallel line in front of us, to call the register for their new class pupils to stand up upon name call, and walk towards and stand behind them in line.

My form tutor on that day was Mr Davidson; a plump, bearded, somewhat camp man with a very operatic sounding voice. He could not have known the effect his words would have had on me in later life.

When he read the register out, it went something like this ….

" Emma Sampson ? "," *present Sir* ", "John Stevenson ? ", "*present Sir*", "David Smith ? ", "*present Sir* ","And who do we have here.........? William Edward Arthur Want- Sibley?".

At this point the entire year of kids' and teachers' burst out laughing… I remember feeling immediately so insecure and in fact scared.

I hardly knew anyone, and yet I had been suddenly thrust into the limelight of ridicule on day one of this new school, and it got far worse. Every first morning and lunchtime registration, the form teacher and all the pupils chanted my name in unison when it was read out.

This ridicule also happened pretty much every day during random corridor encounters I had with pupils and sometimes even teaching staff, throughout the whole of my five year secondary education without let up. I was totally blunted, is all I can say.

For five years I was just hiding, I felt it was safer to be hidden in the shadows and ignored than be recognised and ridiculed. I literally hated waking up on school days and dreading of what the day had in store.

It was brutal and I never told my parents about the bullying, I would just try and skip off school whenever I could.

My father had an identical twin brother Derek, and Uncle Derek was the kindest most compassionate man I've ever known. He was born very ill with a hole in his heart.

My grandmother Ethel, told me that in those days there were no scans, so you never knew exactly how many you could be birthing and the mid- wife thought it was just the one baby, being my father, but she then remarked " *hang on, I think there's another* ", Derek came out very weak and small and the mid- wife said he wouldn't live, so placed the child under a pillow in the corner of the room to die, but when the mid- wife left the room my grandmother suckled him and he survived.

Ethel grew up in Bethnal Green in the East end of London. She was a good pianist and would play rag-time and boogie woogie in the local pubs. She was a strong woman and even in her eighties would greet me with a big bear hug, lifting my feet off the floor when I arrived at her home for Sunday lunch, and this was when I was working on building sites so I was no lightweight either. My dad, Uncle Derek, James and I would make a pilgrimage to her house every Sunday for a feast of home-made sausage rolls, roast dinner with a huge Yorkshire pudding followed by home-made apple pie and clotted cream – enough calories to fuel an Olympic decathlon for a week.

We would crash out on the chairs and settee like a pride of over fed lions whilst she sat knitting and watching 'Songs of Praise'.

She lived to a hundred, and on her birthday I hired a chauffeur- driven Rolls Royce to take her and my brother and I around the East End to see the sites of her past including her old house in Southgate Road, where she stood at the front gate, looked up at the sky and told me how she recalled the first world war Zeppelin Airship bombing raids. She said she recalled a horrific site of an airship that had been shot down over the East End and men falling from the sky.

After the tour we took her to the Ritz Hotel in Mayfair for afternoon tea, and she cracked up laughing because James and I had forgotten to wear ties, which was compulsory in the Ritz, so the concierge lent us ones which didn't exactly make us feel comfortable, and they didn't match our shirt colours either.

I loved her laugh, it was so rich and infectious. Sadly two weeks after her birthday she fell over kicking her cat "Rusty" out the backdoor and broke her hip, was admitted to hospital, and died soon after.

Derek was a very weak child and my father would carry him up the stairs at school on his back, but he had one of the first pioneering heart operations, aged around thirty , which was only meant to last ten years, but he went on to live a healthy life until he died of a sudden heart attack aged sixty seven, he just keeled over on the corner of a street as he was walking with a friend.

He knew he was ill for some time, but never told anybody because he couldn't stand the thought of open heart surgery again. He would take James and I out when our parents were fighting and we'd sometimes stay at his flat.

He was so generous and when I was thirteen he began to teach me to drive in pub car parks and on industrial estates.

He gave me my first car, a 1967 British racing green mini, registration JEL 787E and I began to skip school to either work on it or just take off for a drive, somewhere far from home like Cambridge or Southend Sea front. I had a citizen band (CB) radio fitted in it and my code name or "handle" was "Green Jelly Bean " after the car.

Eventually the school found out and I got summoned to the headmaster with my father and a policeman to caution me, but it didn't stop me, and my father didn't really care, I was a better driver than my mother. She stalled her car on the outside lane of the A10 dual carriageway once, which was petrifying for me and my mate Kevin, in the car with her at the time. In fact, I collected my dad from Victoria station, which is a good hour's drive through the busy streets of London, on one occasion aged fourteen. Eventually the police did catch me out on the road and I was prosecuted for under age driving and as soon as I got my provisional driving licence, aged seventeen, I had a three month suspension.

The bullying at school had an adverse effect on my relationship with my parents and my mother in particular. She was a stunning looking lady, glamorous and many other mothers' in our street were envious of her as she also spoke with good diction.

This caused me problems every time she stood at our garden gate each evening to call me in. I was the posh kid in the street and again got picked on by other lads. I began to resent her and this had a detrimental effect on our relationship down the line, I just didn't make the effort to see her that often.

Both my parents were quite heavy drinkers and would polish off a large bottle of whiskey every night between them. My father would come home from the pub after work, have his dinner around nine pm, which gave my brother and I about half an hour with him before we had to go to bed. Often our sleep was interrupted by my father playing classical music loudly, as he sat in an armchair which he had dragged from the living room into the garden, where he drank his whiskey alone in dark contemplation.

My mother would try and get him to come in, or turn the music down but he would ignore her and eventually we would have angry neighbours banging on our front door. Many years later, during a heart to heart with my father, I was able to gently persuade him to confide in me what it was that had been haunting him all these years?

My mother once told me that he broke down whilst watching a documentary on the Malayan war, but he refused to tell her why. During his national service he was a communications radio operator in the Royal Air force, and posted with a group of commandos, who were sent into the jungle.

As he began to recount an event, he broke down and said *"no William I can't say anymore"*, I reassured him and told him I didn't care what it is, I will always love him no matter what, and that this issue has obviously been a huge burden on him.

He then told me that the group of soldiers he was with on that day came under attack from villagers and that my father unintentionally shot an unarmed young man dead.

I was in tears as he sobbed his heart out like I have never seen, he had been racked with guilt since that traumatic event and had never received any form of post military counselling. This is why he had those dark reflective moments which caused problems with the relationship between my parents over many years. They would argue and fight a lot, which got so bad that their marriage had to end when I was around seventeen.

My mother eventually moved out to live with a friend my father knew and my father had a breakdown and went to live with my grandmother. This left me and James living on our own in the family house.

I left school at sixteen and vowed never to be bullied again. I changed my name to Bill and insisted everyone, including my family and friends, call me by that title, everyone eventually did except my father, who called me Wills.

I was an angry and insecure youth at that time, I felt I had been robbed of an education and had little hope of a successful career and that anger got me into a lot of fights- I was very volatile.

When I left school I began work as a hod carrier (a building site labourer who carried bricks and mortar for bricklaying gangs) .

It was hard graft, but I enjoyed it . My brother got a job as a sales assistant in Dixons the electrical store.

We were very short of money and wouldn't have got by without a friend of mine called Dean moving in with us. Dean was about nineteen at that time and his parents lived about thirty doors up from us in the Barrow Close "the Church Army housing end of our street ".

He was naturally thin and also very fit, he could run a marathon without training even though he smoked forty cigarettes a day. I recall one time when a friend of ours called Joe, challenged Dean to a race from Winchmore Hill to Wood Green tube station and back, which was approximately four miles downhill to Wood Green and of course uphill on the return leg. At that time, both of them were in their thirties.

Now, Joe was a kung foo instructor and fitness fanatic and of course very confident he would win the bet. However, Joe gave up on the return leg and Dean returned to Winchmore Hill hardly out of breath.

Dean was also without doubt the most accident prone person I have ever met, seriously. His mother Stella still thinks he has a death wish to this day.

As an example, one night he came home drunk aged around nineteen, and walked through his parents kitchen back door, through the lounge past his mum and dad sat watching TV, said goodnight and went upstairs to his room. He felt sick, leaned out his bedroom window and fell out onto the shed below, walked back through the kitchen back door and through the lounge past his mum and dad a second time, who didn't bat an eye lid.

I could write a short book just about his mishaps. There are many funny stories about him, however the sad thing was Dean and his father were always fighting and I mean proper punch ups between them.

Eventually during one of their scraps, his dad clumped him over the head with a glass ashtray and as a result, in his early twenties Dean came to live with us.

He was a prolific shop lifter and would steal pretty much anything to order from high street shops, including tennis rackets, expensive clothes, video recorders and even one time a brand new racing bike from a bike shop. His boldness had no limitation.

If we were hungry, he would go and pinch food as well. I also have to admit there were occasions where I did what I had to do to earn the money we needed to get by, sometimes pinching plant and machinery to sell, or on occasion I'd go along with Dean and act as a blocker so that as he walked out of a store, I'd walk in past him to prevent him getting grabbed by security, and I'd take back the clothes he had nicked to the same store, but in a different town and collect the vouchers from a refund to buy our food shopping. Dean's natural running abilities came in good use on a couple of occasions when security tried to catch him, and eventually he did get caught by an off duty detective who was sat in his car in the town car park waiting for his wife. Dean was hiding a stash of nicked goods behind a bush to retrieve later and the detective grabbed him. He never stole another thing after that.

Those were very tough times; and the house resembled an Oliver Twist Fagin's Grotto with all the nicked gear lying about.

We had no central heating so we slept fully clothed and I recall one cold February, the windows in the kitchen froze over on the inside. I left a pint of milk out on the worktop after making a cup of tea, when I returned an hour later to make another, the milk had frozen solid. When I placed it back in the fridge, it eventually thawed out. I could only deduce that the house was in fact colder than the inside of the fridge!

I also recall we couldn't afford to pay an outstanding electricity bill, so the energy company installed a meter which took fifty pence pieces and pound coins. We broke it the afternoon it was installed, and just kept feeding the meter with the same fifty pence piece.

When the man came to empty it two months later, I told him we had a party the night before and someone must have broken into it. I don't think he believed me but he must have took pity on us because he just repaired it and then left us alone.

After a long and acrimonious court battle, my parents got divorced and the house was sold. Both my brother and I were given £2000 each. I was nineteen and James was seventeen . My brother went and lived in shared accommodation and I rented a small one bed flat with my girlfriend at the time, Suzanne.

By now I had enrolled myself in Tottenham Technical college to learn bricklaying . I became good at it, I was neat and fast at laying bricks.

I had a small pick-up truck and started to advertise for building small extensions. Things were good for a while and then the recession of the 1990s kicked in and many bricklayers were out of work and a lot of firms went under.

I was working on a site in Wood Green, North London when the bricklaying contractor went bust.

The foreman turned up with our wage packets one morning as we were about to start work, and said *"sorry fellas, here's your money; there's no more work for you, our firm's gone bust"*.

I was gutted, but seized the moment and went up to the site office without anyone knowing and spoke with the quantity surveyor. I told him that all the bricklayers outside, were in fact working for me and that I had been sub-contracting to the company that had gone bust.

He believed me and I began receiving work direct from this large Construction Company and many more followed.

By the time I was twenty six, I had grown a business that employed over a hundred bricklayers. The profit on the work was very tight though as we were still in recession and I looked to move into commercial building maintenance. I rented offices in Southgate and sub-let part of it out to a Chartered Building Surveyor, Mark Blooman. I met Mark on a Landmark Education self-development course called the Forum, which I was invited to go on by a Cypriot Architect I had made acquaintance with, a lovely guy called George Popadopoulos. He owned a large commercial building in Bethnal Green that he was converting into apartments. He wanted to award me the project, but he felt that I would be easier to work with if I aligned with his personal development beliefs. I remember thinking at the time that I didn't care if he wanted me to walk around with a fish hanging out of my pocket and a Viking helmet on my head, so long as I won the project. I did find the course very empowering and realised how much of an effect the first day of secondary school had on my life. The insecurity I felt and need to earn respect had shaped my career and the anger I had towards my mother for the bullying I had experienced during those school years had caused me to distance myself from her.

Mark and I hit it off, he has the same sense of humour as I, and he supported me by reading over any business letters I had to write, correcting them or in most cases re-writing them so they had a more professional impression.

Success in business gave me a tremendous feeling of self-respect and I began to gain recognition in the local community.

Suzanne and I got married in 1991, and we later had three children; our daughter Ashleigh, then Luke, then Kane. We were a happy family for many years, I was building a bigger, more successful enterprise and we were eventually living quite a luxurious lifestyle. We had a large six bedroom house in an expensive area, owned a holiday apartment on a golf course in the South of France, had five star holidays, I was driving a black Maserati and we always had plenty of money. It was all a very materialistic way of life in those days.

However, the success came at a price, I found it difficult to switch off and relax, and I couldn't for example sit on the sofa with my wife and kids and watch TV.

I had to be doing something, I started Jiu Jitsu and within three years I was a black belt, then I trained in boxing, I had drumming lessons, did my motorbike test, even passed a day skipper course so I was licensed to pilot an eighty foot motor boat, then piano lessons which I got surprisingly quite good at.

Those were all activities to occupy the moments after work when I couldn't be still. Oh, and I forgot one, I also played rugby at weekends and later down the line as my business grew, I even had my own company rugby team made up of managers and tradesmen who worked for me.

In 1999 I took the family on holiday to Turkey for a week. Just before we left I'd met with Spencer

Oliver an ex professional boxer who I wanted to hire to coach me to train me for amateur white collar fights. It was a period when, without doubt I was the fittest I had ever been. We agreed that upon my return, I'd begin at his gym in Finchley. However, on the last day of the holiday, I called one of the directors of my company to check in and he said I needed to speak to my brother. My mother had been rushed to hospital, she had collapsed. The next morning I went straight to the hospital and my mother was sat up in bed with an oxygen mask on, she was very jaundiced and weak due to liver failure, we stayed as long as we could, but it was very difficult.

I had not been close to her during my adult years and I was really struggling with guilt. The next day when James and I arrived at her bedside, she didn't look any better. She was sat up in bed but her breathing was laboured, still wearing the oxygen mask strapped to her face.

We had only been in her room ten minutes, when these buzzers sounded, medical staff rushed in and told us we had to leave. We waited outside and it wasn't long before we were told that she was being taken into intensive care. Her organs were shutting down and by the time we were able to go and see her, she was unconscious. I asked one of the nurses if she thought she would pull through and she shook her head.

James and I were trying hard to hold it together and support our mother, we sat next to her talking to her for eight hours and watched as the monitors gradually ticked down. Her heartbeat and blood pressure all dropping minute by minute and eventually the nurse said" she's gone".

At that exact point my mother's arm suddenly shot up in the air and dropped back on the bed as if to flag up, she could hear us !

I was absolutely devastated, I had so much guilt inside me it was terrible, I had so many regrets for not having a better relationship with her, for not at least making an effort and seeing her more often, it was truly awful. James and I took our mother's ashes to the Channel Island of Jersey, where in her younger years' she had been a beauty queen in a pageant. We scattered them on a rock overlooking Corbiere beach.

By 2007 my business had grown into a £6.5m turnover PLC and employed over one hundred and thirty people including my father, my brother James and of course Dean. I was at the top of my game and even had an article published about me in the Times newspaper Business section.

However I recall feeling very unhappy deep inside, I was disconnected, I had no real friends, they were either business acquaintances or clients that I needed to befriend.

I had begun to drink more, partly because I was out entertaining clients twice a week and partly to block these feelings of disconnection and insecurity. I was always worried about losing it all.

Around 2009 I was beginning to receive requests for advice from other businessmen and I was introduced to a very wealthy night club owner who had been having difficulties with his business partner.

I ended up co-ordinating a high court action with barristers and lawyers and he was ultimately handed sole ownership of the night club group.

We became good friends and shortly after that I became his CEO and with the assistance of my own accountant Heather, ran all the finances and operations of his multi-million pound company which consisted of four venues, one of which was a two thousand capacity club.

The group employed thirty doormen and I quickly learned that these were very hard, dangerous and connected men indeed, and I'll leave it at that!

The night club world is not for the faint hearted, drugs and violence go with the territory as does the notoriety and ego which only distanced me further from my family.

Success in business can sometimes attract attention from a criminal element that look for opportunities to collect contractually disputed debts.

I had my fair share of these thugs over the years and as I was the figure head of my business, invariably it was me personally that got targeted and there was more than one occasion when there were serious threats on my life, causing an enormous amount of stress for me and the family.

Add that to the pressures of actually running my own business and four night clubs for someone else and I had now begun to have severe panic attacks, my release was to drink more.

By the time the financial crises hit in 2010 my marriage was breaking down, I had to move out in March 2011. I didn't cope with it well and I have regrets around how I dealt with things.

The bank had begun to withdraw the million pound facility I had, and I was struggling to keep my own business going, so I left the night club position to focus on my own crisis hit operation but bit by bit my business shrank to a point where ultimately I handed the last remaining part of the operation to a much larger company to save as many jobs as I could.

I was in a bad way, I was living on my own in a flat in St Albans. Cut off and isolated from my family, with very few friends and relying on my best mate Barry for support to get me through the day. Barry and I met through work, he was head of building maintenance in a large retailer and my company was an approved contractor on his repair network. However, Barry and I got on so well that I decided to stop working for this retailer to ensure our relationship was never compromised by business.

I know it's a cliché, but he really is like a brother to me and my late father even stated this to one of his close friends, but even Barry had no idea how bad a state I was getting myself into. I guess I felt embarrassed to tell him, I'd lost my business and made bad investments with the remaining life savings, my wife was divorcing me and my drinking was out of control.

I found it difficult to leave the flat because of crippling panic attacks which were accompanied by hot sweats and a paralysing inability to be in the company of others. Most days I was drinking five bottles of wine a day, half a bottle of brandy and even a couple of pints of larger.

At night when I eventually got into bed, I had to have a glass of wine on my bedside table, for when I woke, to go to the toilet, I could drink it to try and get back off to sleep. Eventually I had to get sleeping pills.

Every morning I'd lie in bed alone not having slept much at all. Sometimes in tears and suffering from a morbid state of depression, it was a living hell and on the morning of July 3, 2012 I was seriously considering taking my own life.

By 10am that day I had already drunk my first bottle of wine and I was disgusted with myself. What had I become, what had I lost and why is this happening to me?

I don't know to this day why I called my brother James, we had grown apart by now, we rarely saw each other, mainly I think due to the fact that he had worked for me and this put pressure on our relationship, I don't recall what I said to him, but within a very short period of time, he was ringing my doorbell.

I was sobbing uncontrollably at this point.

He took me to the Priory in Southgate, a private run recovery centre.

Upon arrival I was assessed by the centre manager during which time, I couldn't even speak, I'd just given up and no longer wanted to exist.

The doctor took blood samples and did all the necessary checks, and I was given a vitamin B jab and put on Librium which is a strong sedative. The centre placed me under 24hour suicide watch, I wasn't allowed outside the building and throughout the night, nurses would open my bedroom door and call my name to make sure I was ok. I was cut off from the outside world completely for the next fourteen days, no mobile phone, no visitors and I wasn't allowed to call anyone.

The first four days of my residency in the Priory are a blur, I don't recall much because of the effect Librium had on me but I was sobering up and with counselling, I was feeling better.

I attended an Alcoholics Anonymous Meeting (AA) in the centre grounds and this was a turning point. A guy called Paddy came and spoke with me in the garden after the meeting. Although he had an Irish sounding name, he spoke in a gravelly London accent. He'd been in AA for over ten years and was sponsoring two other members.

He said I needed a sponsor to help me through the twelve steps and that he would introduce me to his mate Pete who would sponsor me. Pete had also been a member of AA for over a decade. Before he left, Paddy gave me words of advice I'll never forget.

He said " *don't go into your own head without two responsible adults holding both your hands*! " What he meant was, try not to reflect on the past and how you ended up where you are now.

I continued attending weekly AA meetings when I left the Priory at a church in Winchmore Hill, ironically round the corner from Barrow Close where I grew up. I embarked on the twelve steps process which calls for one to completely make amends for any hurt you had caused others. This requires you to write a list of all those people and next to their names, where you felt responsibility for causing hurt or upset. You then need to contact them and humbly apologise or do whatever you can to make amends.

This can be done in person or by letter.

I met Suzanne in person and at Kings Cross station hotel. I had no outcome in mind other than to sincerely apologise and take responsibility for my part of our breakup and by December 2012 we were divorced.

The twelve steps of AA are a very enlightening and empowering process and by the end of it you have a meeting with your AA sponsor.

Pete reviewed my list and when we were both satisfied I'd completed them thoroughly, he forgave me and told me to burn the list.

That's it, that's how it worked and I have to say I felt unburdened. I praise the AA for the important work they do and the support they offer people who find themselves addicted to drink, however, eventually after twelve months I felt uncomfortable being made to feel, by some, that it was a disease and that you must for the rest of your life attend meetings and be committed to abstaining from alcohol.

I came to my own conclusion that it was more important to deal with the underlying issues that drove a person to drink, and in my case it was to block out the pain of losing everything and only when I truly came to terms with that, would I have a different relationship with alcohol. Today I would only drink in the evenings and never touch spirits, just a few beers and I like the socialising that goes with it.

Of course you can't be in AA if you drink and on my final meeting , when it was my turn to share with the room how I had been doing over the past seven days, I confessed that I had drunk a couple of bottles of beer in that time. You could have heard a pin drop , then a lady spoke out and said she had had a couple of glasses of wine and then another member admitted that he had had a drink.

The chairman said I would have to hand over the sobriety chips, which were aluminium coins of different colours which are given for each month you stay sober. Basically he said I would have to start over again.

After the meeting I called Pete my sponsor and explained what had happened and said I'm eternally grateful for his support over the past twelve months and that I was fine but didn't want to stay in AA anymore. He totally understood.

However, it was in AA that I accepted that there was a power greater than myself, a Spirit energy and I would pray every morning and every evening to it before I went to sleep.

It was a great comfort and I actually noticed my prayers were being answered and actioned. I felt liberated after what I had been through and changed my name to "Will ". It was difficult for those who had known me as Bill to accept this and to this day my brother and ex-wife still call me Bill, but my father was happy.

My father eventually met his second wife, a lovely Irish lady called Jane.

They adored each other and were inseparable. My father was a bit of an eccentric and add that to the fact he looked the spitting image of Prince Charles and had a posh voice, made him a very colourful and popular character. A very wise man, but also a bit intolerant, sometimes opinionated, but always fun and jolly. Jane loved his company and laughed at him with equal devotion.

Before I left Alcoholics Anonymous, and on the evening of Monday, March 18 2013 I had just come out of the AA meeting , turned my phone on and there was a voice message from Jane, saying she was worried about my father. I called her and she was in tears saying he was seriously ill but he wouldn't accept that he was and she couldn't get him to the doctor.

My father and Jane lived in a beautiful Victorian seaside town called Broadstairs, in the county of Kent. A very picture post card town where Charles

Dickens liked to holiday. He wrote the "Pickwick Papers" and "Nicholas Nickleby " there. It's a two hour drive from London and I drove down early the next morning.

My father was sat up in bed eating a small amount of fruit. When I walked into the bedroom he said cheerfully " hello Wills " . I asked him how he was feeling and what's going on. He said *"oh, for god's sake it's just a kidney infection, I'm fine and she should stop making all this bloody fuss"*.

We chatted for a while and he said he was just about to get up and get dressed, and we'll go for a drink.

I went back into the lounge with Jane and she was very teary, she had heard what he said and she told me she was finding blood around the place and in his trousers, that he refused to give her a urine sample the doctor had requested.

On one occasion he gave her the sample bottle, which had water in it, she told him that wasn't urine, which he denied immediately saying it was and so to prove it she drank it in front of him. Both of us laughed for a moment, but I knew he was very sick and looked jaundiced.

I recall feeling quite composed at this time, I was present, I was sober and able to be there for my father and Jane. My brother came down the next day, but couldn't stay as he was coming down with a bad chest infection.

My father deteriorated very quickly and by the Thursday and Friday of that week he was in very severe pain.

As I sat with him on the Friday afternoon, just the two of us in the Royal Albion pub whilst he sipped a small glass of beer waiting for Jane to arrive, I said

" look mate, you're dying , you know it and I know it, but it doesn't have to be so painful , please let me take you to hospital so they can at least give you pain killers".

He was very quiet and just looked at me, then he slowly nodded. I got him admitted the next morning, by which time he was in the foetal position with the pain and by that afternoon he had passed away.

The last time I spoke with him, he was lying in bed asleep , I went over to him, stroked his head and gave him four kisses, one from me and one for each of my children, I said goodbye dad, turned and walked to the door.

I turned back to look at him and he opened his eyes , waved at me and said "bye Wills" as if we were going to see each other again.

That was the last time I saw him alive, he died moments later and my ears immediately began to ring with tinnitus.

My father and I were very close, he'd supported the transition I'd embarked upon and he knew how tough things had been for me. I can reflect on his passing and appreciate that I was in a much more stable emotional condition and although I was saddened by losing him, I felt proud of how I was able to support him during his last few days.

By this time, I had moved to a lovely apartment in Hertford overlooking a river and my son Luke had moved in with me. On my birthday that year 27 August, 2013 I had my first profound spiritual experience, it scared the life out of me and I remember it very vividly.

It was a warm summer's night, my bedroom balcony doors were open.

I had brought a cup of cocoa to bed with me, said my prayers and as I was about to turn the table lamp off, I suddenly saw a long dark shadow fly out from the corner of my room, over the ceiling and down under my bed. I would say it was about one meter in length and not very wide.

I thought what the hell was that, and actually said out loud "what are you? what do you want?" I lay there for a bit waiting for something to happen, but all was very still and I eventually drifted off to sleep.

It was around 5:30 am that I began to hear the ducks and geese on the river, there was one particular goose different from all the others called a barnacle goose, it had a very distinctive and quite loud 'honk', and as I was listening, eyes closed to this dawn chorus, I suddenly heard and felt my duvet cover quickly lift up next to me and this energy came and lay on top of me, pinning me to the bed.

I was absolutely petrified, I couldn't call out and I couldn't move, I couldn't open my eyes and I felt as if my Spirit inside was trying to wrestle with it, I was saying the Lord's Prayer in my mind, but it continued to just lay on me. In the end I recall just submitting and completely let go, I thought there is nothing I can do and as I did that I felt relaxation and it left me.

There have been many more incredible experiences that I have had during the early hours and even in broad daylight which I will tell you about later.

By 2014 my savings had run out, I had been self-supporting my outgoings whilst investing finances in the new antimicrobial product I was trying to launch with other investors, and there was no sign of a return as yet and in fact this business was being compromised by the other three directors, my investment was in jeopardy, I had to vacate the apartment in Hertford, and even borrow money from Barry to survive. Luke moved back to his mother's and I relocated into shared accommodation.

My landlady was Brenda, she was in her seventies and had very strong Christian beliefs. Her late husband Denis was a minister and together they had a vision to build a Christian community centre in Nigeria, and Brenda continued to develop this and raise funds for the project even though she had a heart condition which meant she couldn't fly to visit the site anymore. I've seen images of this centre and it is huge. Amazing what some people can achieve.

Brenda had a large house with a river running through the bottom of the garden overlooking fields. It was a lovely peaceful setting but I literally had one double bedroom and shared the facilities with her and another lodger, Jay who was a school teacher. It was hard to comprehend living in shared accommodation but I was determined to stay positive and look to make the best out of the situation. I introduced a Monday cooking night where one of us would cook for the other three.

Brenda loved this and we enjoyed those evenings. Christmas 2015 I was on my own and had nowhere to go so I enrolled with Crises at Christmas which is a charity that provides venues for the homeless to receive meals including a Christmas dinner. There are also activities, treatments and advice from doctors, dentists , hairdressers and they will find people beds for the nights. I worked Christmas Eve and Christmas Day and the day after Boxing Day.

I was on the door at the centre and greeted guests and would assist with serving the diners (137 of them on Christmas Day) and on occasions work the café which gave out free drinks and biscuits, etc. I have to say it was one of the best Christmas's I have ever had and I would thoroughly recommend it.

This was however, another very difficult time, I had to adjust and accept that I had lost everything and gone right back to square one.

I believe that if I hadn't have been able to rely on my spiritual beliefs at that time, I would have gone into depression again.

I needed to find work quick and my brother suggested I try to get on board with a firm he was getting consultancy domestic insurance claims surveys.

I was perfect for the role, my construction company had done a lot of insurance work in its day, I was good with people and I had experience of valuing repairs. The income started off very slowly to begin with, but I really enjoyed the work and gradually I began to find financial income security.

By this time, I had to find a lawyer to assist me to recover monies from the other business I had invested my life savings in.

The Insurance Claims Company I was contracting from asked if I would go to Northern Ireland to cover for a surveyor who was on leave.

I was happy to assist and I worked a week based in Belfast covering the whole of the territory.

I was amazed at how beautiful the country was. I had only ever seen news footage of Belfast and heard about the "troubles", I had no idea how stunning the landscape was around it or indeed how friendly the people were. County Antrim has the second most picturesque coastal road in the whole of Europe and I loved working there.

A second opportunity arose shortly after that due to the business being inundated with storm claims, so again I was delighted to relocate for a week, this time I found myself in Carrickfergus staying in the most haunted hotel in the whole of the UK called Dobbins Inn.

During one of those nights, I had the same energy visit me in the early hours, and it gently turned me over from sleeping on my side to my back, I wasn't as afraid this time.

The claims work involved surveying people's homes who had either suffered some form of escape of water damage, storm damage, accidental or impact.

Back in England my role was to detail the damage and assist in settling the claim on behalf of insurers. I therefore met many homeowners in my working day and I recall a customer who was in a hurry because she had a Reiki treatment to go to, I had no idea what Reiki was so I asked and she replied it helps with her tinnitus.

My ears had been ringing like mad for months, since the day my father died and when it was really bad I would have to put background music on at night to help me sleep. I asked her if I could have her therapist's number and she gave it to me. Later that day I called the therapist, Nicola Novack, and explained why I wanted to see her.

Nicola lived in Mill Hill, North London in a lovely big house. She had one of her ground floor reception rooms converted to a treatment room, and after a brief chat she asked me to lay on the bed face up, she put background music on, told me to close my eyes and simply relax.

It felt amazing, so relaxing and I could feel this warmth as her hands hovered over me and when she brought me back she asked if my mother smoked? I was a bit surprised but said yes she did, and she said, well, your mother and father were both here, and they were telling her what I been through and what I had lost, she knew about my company and about my parents both being big drinkers. I was quite emotional during this reading because there is no way Nicola could have known this, and it planted a seed of interest in mediumship.

The tinnitus subsided a bit but later down the line I've learnt that this is a common condition with those that are awakening, it's like you become hyper sensitive to this planet's vibration and your inner ear picks up on it, the more I got used to it and accepted it, the less it bothered me.

I was given a book called the Celestine Prophecy by a friend which I found spellbinding, it's a novel written by James Redfield and it contains spiritual messages and guidance within an adventure storyline.

It inspired me to go to Hertford Spiritualist church one Sunday to see a demonstration of platform mediumship.

I recall being sat in this small hall with about thirty others watching the medium.

After several sweeps of readings with the congregation, she then turned to me and said "*I have your mum here , and she's crying for you, she says you have lost everything and that it had to happen and that she is showing me a present, a gift to give you*"..

I have to admit, I don't recall everything the medium said but again I was receiving compelling evidence of afterlife.

In October 2015, the UK was hit by a big storm which affected the Midlands, Manchester, and Bolton area.

I was asked to assist in the area and drove up to stay in the Bolton Macron Stadium Hotel.

There were other surveyors there, colleagues including my brother James. We were all very busy during the day and in the evenings we would just hang out in the hotel bar, which I didn't enjoy much. The two directors of the company, really lovely guys, that were providing us with the insurance claims work invited myself and the other surveyors out for a Chinese meal one night as a thank you for all our efforts and during the meal, I asked one of them how things were in Northern Ireland.

He replied that they were struggling, they desperately needed another surveyor and that he was due to go over for interviews next month.

I don't know why I commented in this way, but I felt a strong urge to say *" well I might fancy a change of scene"*. He said *" Will if you would go there, that would be brilliant "*. I remember feeling quite surprised by this discussion and thinking , what the hell was I talking about, I'm not going to work and live in Northern Ireland, so I said to him " ok, let me think about it, I'll talk to my sons, they might not be too keen ".

The next night , I decided I didn't want to spend it in the hotel and googled spiritual churches in Bolton. Up popped one, and it so happened there was a meeting that night so I decided to go along.

It was a much bigger venue than Hertford with around eighty in the congregation and when the medium came on, you could tell she was very experienced. I sat around the fourth row from the front, arms folded just observing, but she then turned to me and said;

"I'm with the gentlemen in the blue shirt with his arms crossed, I've got your mum with me, she's a glamorous lady, and she's crying tears of frustration for you because she had to watch you lose it all and she couldn't intervene, she's telling me this had to happen, but that they are building you back up brick by brick, that you're going to be given a gift and you will know what it is when you get it. Your dad's also here and he is showing me a steering wheel of a car, perhaps you're going on a journey?"

The medium then paused for a moment as if she was listening on what was to be said next and then she spoke " And your mum's telling me your destiny is staring you in the face ." another pause " It's staring you in the face !". Wow, I thought, this must be Northern Ireland.

I spoke to Luke and Kane when I returned to London about the possibility of relocating for a while to Northern Ireland and both of my boys were just so supportive, they both said, they didn't care where I lived so long as they could get to see me and that I was happy.

On Valentine's day, 2016 I said goodbye to my landlady Brenda and set off from London in my BMW 5 Series with all my worldly possessions, as well as my fifteen year old son Kane.

We left in the early hours, drove to Liverpool and caught the seven hour ferry to Belfast. I had secured a rental on a stunning apartment overlooking the Belfast Lough and Carrickfergus Castle, just fifteen minutes North of Belfast in County Antrim. It was a three double bedroom dwelling with a balconied lounge and stunning views. To this day, the sun rise and sun sets outside my window take my breath away.

After Kane went back home on the Sunday afternoon, I was literally on my own, I didn't know anybody whatsoever.

I decided to take a walk to the local Rugby Club, from my many experiences of this environment, you'll always find someone friendly to talk to. As I ordered my first pint at the bar, a gentlemen next to me said *" you from England are ye ?"*.

Ray was a guy in his late fifties, a local in Carrick all his life and his mate Pete was around the same age, but was originally from England and had lived in Carrick for forty years. Between the pair of them, I didn't buy a drink all afternoon, we had really good banter between us and we exchanged numbers.

They were both colourful characters and successful businessmen.

Ray was apparently the 1977 disco dancing champion of Northern Ireland, he would text or call me virtually every day for the first few weeks to check I was ok and if I needed any advice. On my fiftieth birthday in 2017, I had a big birthday bash at the Windrose night club and restaurant overlooking Carrick Marina, with a DJ playing all my 70s and 80s era tunes. Everyone was up dancing and we witnessed Ray spin round and drop to a splits on the floor, how he never ended up in hospital is beyond me. He tried hard to hide the grimace of pain which he immediately displayed, as his traumatised hamstrings reminded him why he had stopped performing that move many years ago.

I felt excited, to have re-located to a new land , it was liberating in itself to be honest, because for the first time in my life, I could literally re-invent myself, be my true self, my life was a blank page ready to be written, a new beginning.

I joined a gym and engaged a personal trainer Davey and I also wanted to find a spiritual church or organisation.

I wasn't sure if this would be even something available in Belfast and when I googled spiritualism, up popped a Reiki Master, Paul Deveney. That's interesting I thought?

He was running a six month Reiki Mastership course. I felt drawn to this, if only to meet others, and I enrolled.

Awakening

I'm going to fast forward this journey for a moment. I've just completed the first chapter of the book, and I knew it would be the hardest to write, so I celebrated by taking my girlfriend Julianne (Jules) off to one of our favourite beauty spots on the North Antrim coast called Ballygally. It's an area of outstanding natural beauty and where I finished the first chapter at a small window table overlooking the sea in the Ballygally Castle Hotel.

The castle dates back to the 17th century and is reputed to be one of the most haunted places in all of Ireland and has featured in the Game of Thrones series.

When I finished writing, we went to a local pub called Mattie's Meeting House a mile or so up the road.

This is a very traditional, no frills northern Irish local with two small nook bars and a larger one. We stepped into the smallest and were greeted by three gentlemen, one of whom was sat on a stool with his right leg stretched out at right angles resting on another stool in front of him, he looked in great discomfort. Now it doesn't take Jules or me very long to strike up a conversation with strangers as we both love meeting new people.

As I was ordering us both a pint of Guinness, Jules was asking what was wrong with his leg and he replied that he had been in agony for months, he spent hundreds on physiotherapy but nobody knows what's wrong with him.

I began to feel the energy throbbing in my left palm and the finger tips on my right hand were emitting wires of energy towards him, my Spirit guides were here ,"blending with me" and obviously keen to treat this man , I spoke out " *I can get rid of that for you* " he just looked at me and said "*what was that ?*" I said " *I'm a healer and I can get rid of that pain now for you if you like ?* " Jules said "*yes he can* ". He said he would try anything and as I crossed the small bar the other guys stepped aside and I placed a stool next to him and sat down to begin. I placed my left palm behind his back about six inches away from his body and my right hand hovered under his thigh.

The Spirit guides began to blend with me, I felt the familiar cobweb like energy gently come from behind my head and around my face. In a few moments he went quiet and I could feel the full force of the wires of energy being projected into his leg. Whilst this was happening I could hear Jules chatting away to the other regulars.

After about ten minutes, he began to lift his leg and bend his knee in discomfort, almost contort . I've seen this happen before when I've treated people for sciatica.

After about 15 – 20 minutes I felt my guides withdraw their energy and this is a sign that they have done what they needed to do. I asked him to stand up and the pain had gone. However, I felt the need to tell him it would get worse before it gets betters. I also know that there was a lot of emotional healing being given to him.

He was in his mid-sixties and looked fairly fit, he was an ex- policeman and had three children, two by his first marriage, that were in their thirties and a young son who was only eight from his second partner. He told me that he absolutely dotes on his young son and has been very sad that he's been unable to take him to his football matches because of the pain he's been in.

A couple of days later I was passing by the Meeting House and dropped in for a pint.

There was a couple in there who knew the guy I did a healing with, and they told me that he had called them afterwards, to tell them what had happened and that he was going to go to the hospital to get checked out. They told me that he had been admitted and operated on to remove a cancerous growth in his hip.

There was a reason Jules and I were in that pub at that time, and it was for that gentleman to receive a healing from Spirit. To give him the courage to face up to getting himself checked out. I've been back a few times and the locals tell me he is doing really well and asks after me and Jules, hopefully we'll get to meet him again soon.

I'll tell you more about these healing experiences later in the book.

Returning to early development and the Reiki course, I still had little knowledge of what Reiki was at that time but now know its similar to spiritual healing in that the practitioner channels a hidden energy, but I never felt guides blend with me in the way they do now. There were about six other students on the first weekend Level One course and at the end of it, the Master gave us the attunement. This mystical initiation connects a student to the universal energies and Spirit guides, to enable this healing energy to be channelled through them. We were invited to practice on each other.

For some reason, I didn't lay hands on, as the others did. My hands were about four to six inches above the person lying on the treatment bed, but I recall feeling a sense of disbelief as I began to feel heat in both my palms.

At the end of the first session, we were advised to meditate every day if we could and to practice healing our Chakras and those of family members. We learnt that there are seven chakras in our body which energy flows through. When these become blocked it can often lead to illness. Each Chakra represents different things. The Root Chakra is based at the base of the spine and represents our foundation and grounding. The Sacral Chakra is located in our lower abdomen and represents a sense of abundance, well-being, pleasure and sexuality. The Solar Plexus chakra is in our upper abdomen and represents self-worth, self-confidence and self-esteem. The Heart Chakra in the centre of the chest is for emotional issues; love, joy and inner peace. The Throat Chakra is our ability to communicate and for self-expression. Its location is in the throat. The Third Eye Chakra is located between the eyes on our forehead and represents intuition, imagination, wisdom and the ability to think and make decisions. Finally, the Crown Chakra is located on the top of the head and represents our ability to be fully connected spiritually. It is quite common to experience emotional clearings after each Level of Reiki. This is part of a cleansing to remove any past upset that may continue to linger in the form of memories which may continue to resurface at times, and block our feelings of serenity and peace. It's important when giving Reiki to someone that the practitioner is able to be present and not distracted by their own emotions, to be a pure channel for the universal healing energy.

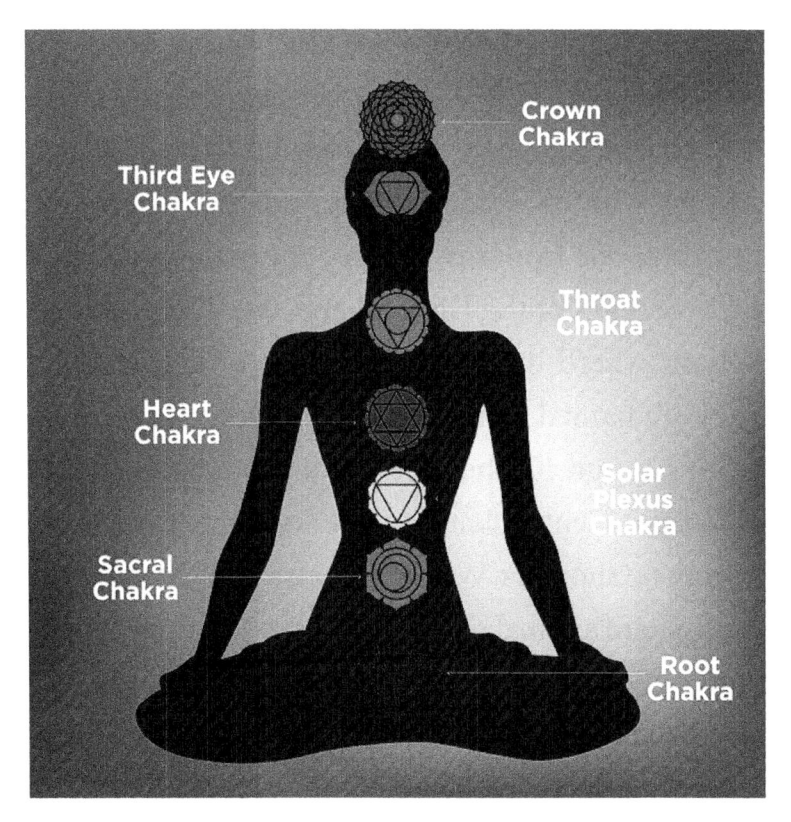

Diagram of a meditating figure showing the seven chakras: Crown Chakra, Third Eye Chakra, Throat Chakra, Heart Chakra, Solar Plexus Chakra, Sacral Chakra, and Root Chakra.

At that time I had no family members around me to practice on and I hardly knew anybody.

However, the people of Carrickfergus are very friendly and they were all fascinated to find that an Englishman had relocated to their "wee town".

The focus of Carrickfergus is the castle, it's where William of Orange landed with his troops and went on to defeat James II.

I can see the castle from my lounge windows and the lough is a wide estuary that runs past the castle and out to the Irish Sea. The Titanic was built in Belfast and on its maiden voyage it set off along this Belfast Lough, I sometimes imagine it sailing past my window, what a sight it must have been and I can also see from my window the statuesque large yellow cranes of the Harland and Wolff ship yard in Belfast, where the doomed liner was constructed. They are named Samson and Goliath.

Just opposite the castle is a Wetherspoon pub called the Central bar, but the locals call it simply "spoons" (short for Wetherspoons). The people who drink there are real characters, I call them the *"loons from spoons"* because they all make me laugh in one way or another. Unfortunately we lost one of them recently.

Billy Haggan died aged sixty seven, from a sudden heart attack on Sunday July 1, 2018. He was a born and raised Carrick man and called the Central bar HQ, short for headquarters and you would be guaranteed to find him there each afternoon, sat at a table holding court with the ladies, dressed sharply with his bottle of favourite white wine. Jules and I loved him and he will be sorely missed. On the morning that he died, I was staying with Jules at her house in Belfast. I awoke, turned to Jules and said, I got a text message image in my mind saying he's dead.

I had no idea who was dead or that it was Billy, and when we went downstairs to the kitchen to get a coffee, I was flicking through the pictures on my phone and found a short clip of Billy and his girlfriend June.

They were out drinking in the sunshine and I videoed them having a laugh as June mimicked Billy's distinctive stroll.

I showed this clip to Jules and then got my things and went back to my place. We had agreed to meet up at 11am that morning at a harbour restaurant which had a lovely position overlooking the castle. Before I met Jules I sat and meditated, called in my spirit guides and as I began to go deeper I felt this light pulse of pain in my neck which travelled down to my chest.

It was distinctive, but not that painful, so didn't think too much of it, but when Jules arrived, I mentioned what I had felt, to her. We had only been sat together for about fifteen minutes when June rang me, in tears.

She had just found Billy dead in bed, he had got up earlier that morning, potted around and went back to bed to read. She went and checked in on him around 10am and he had passed away. I felt Billy around me very strongly that night in my apartment.

I could hear his voice in my mind saying *"ok big man, you were right son, I'm here and I'm sorry for upsetting everyone"* I spoke aloud and told him not to worry Billy it's time for you to go to home mate, we will look after June. He also appeared in my mind when I sat the next morning, wearing cream trousers, a canary yellow polo shirt and a black trilby hat. I met his girlfriend June a few days later in "spoons" and mentioned this to her and she smiled and said she had bought Billy the trousers and polo shirt in those colours on the Friday before he died and when they were out shopping he was looking to buy a hat to. We have since found out from the post mortem that Billy died from a blockage in his garrotted artery on the left side where I felt the sensation.

In the early days, these Carrickfergus locals were all keen to find out about who I was? why I was here? and what I did, and it wasn't long after my Reiki level two attunement that they discovered I did Reiki. I don't know that many of them knew what it was, and simply out of curiosity for some they came to see me for treatments.

The results were amazing and word began to spread.

I recall one lady in particular who was suffering from "graves disease", it's an autoimmune disease that affects the thyroid gland which can cause all manner of problems including bulging eyes and one of hers was.

Treatment is quite radical and ultimately this lady was facing the final stage which is radiotherapy to zap the overactive gland, and the patient is then faced with having to take steroids for the rest of their days.

She had two treatments with me, during the first, she began to cough as I worked on her throat chakra. We learn that it is in our throat chakra where pent up emotional upset can be stored, which in itself can make us ill.

noun: dis-ease
1. **a disorder of structure or function in a human, animal, or plant, especially one that produces specific symptoms or that affects a specific location and is not simply a direct result of physical injury.**

She came to me again a week later and on this occasion, she was more relaxed as she lay on the treatment bed, soft background music playing and my hands were hovering over the various chakra areas sending heat from my palms. Neither of us were prepared for what happened next.

When she came round, she opened her eyes and said she had been seeing images of her ex-partner, they had a son together and following a very acrimonious breakup, she lost custody and for five years had very limited access to her child. She began to cry, which in my view was an emotional release that had to happen. However, the next morning at 7:30am I received a text from her which said *" what have you done to me Will, I haven't stopped crying since I left your place, I've been up all night and I can't go to work !"*

I called her and reassured her she would be ok and that this is a big emotional release for her.

The next day she text me to say she felt amazing. I saw her nine months later at the retail store and she looked so well, her eye had gone back to normal size and she was off medication. I was absolutely astounded.

Reiki can also have an effect on the practitioner causing the clearing of emotional upset and blockages from your past.

These are very common, particularly after each attunement and I recall feeling very down, insecure and alone after Reiki Level 2.

I had begun to attend the Belfast Spiritual Church every now and then to watch the platform mediums' work and one Sunday evening I watched Debbie Griffin.

Debbie is a clairaudient medium and spiritual healer which means she has the incredible ability to perceive sounds or words from the spirit world which are not audible to the normal ear. She can also see images of the deceased in her mind's eye so she can describe those in Spirit world.

Born in Germany, her family relocated to Belfast when she was at an early age, where she remains to this day. On the platform that evening she was very accurate with the information that was being given to her by friends and loved ones of those that had past to spirit to those sat in the congregation.

It was during the emotional clearing I was experiencing after my level 2 Reiki, that I decided I needed to see Debbie for a private reading and so I arranged this with her and met her on the Thursday evening at the Church.

When I arrived, Debbie welcomed me and led me to a small room where we both sat down and whilst I can't recall every word of what she told me, I can recall the following, she said "*I have your mum and dad here, and although they were not together in this life, they both came here today and have settled their differences, I also have other family members with them, she said they are telling me that you are meant to be here and that you have healing, that they know you lost everything, but they are going to assist you, they want you to get back your confidence in business, that you have ideas you've been thinking of lately, that everything will come full circle.*

Your grandfather on your dad's side was a strict, stubborn man and I can see him wagging his finger and his telling me to tell you that you must stick with this, it's very important!.

I never knew my grandad, my dad's dad, but I was told by my grandmother that he was a very stubborn and strict man.

She told me that he fell out with his children, and in particular my father, when they all lived together, so he confined himself to living and sleeping in the backroom for six months. My grandmother would have to serve his dinner to him in the back room, whilst his children and wife ate in the front one.

The reading was just the reassurance I needed and as I drove home I remember feeling so grateful and lucky that I had been able to find a medium who could connect with my deceased parents, it was a great comfort to me.

I'd been romancing about the idea of establishing a healing centre in Carrickfergus and had the name Celestine Centre in mind, I had also been walking past a building which reminded me of my old offices in London, it resembled a bank and it had been up for sale for some time.

It was a bank repossession and nobody would buy it because it had a bad damp problem on the internal ground floor walls, but I had a hunch I knew I could solve the problem cheaply, as I knew the cause was likely to be the badly designed guttering, from my experience as an Insurance claims surveyor.

Within three weeks of the reading with Debbie, I had put an offer in on the building and the bank accepted it. I secured a small mortgage and for the first time in years, I owned real estate, which felt good.

I also set a web-site up called the Celestine Centre as a platform for the healing centre which

I was committed to developing. I have no doubt that my loved ones' in spirit guided me to achieve these things.

I completed my Level 3 Reiki Master course and through word of mouth, I began to get more and more people come to me.

I attended the Spiritualist church more regularly, especially if I knew Debbie Griffin was working platform, it fascinated me how strong her connection was with the spirit world or the other dimension we can't see.

Later that year, I decided to go to the Monday evening Awareness class at the Belfast Spiritualist Church. That's when I met Jules for the first time.

The remarkable thing is that she was also there for the first time. She looked lovely and I felt drawn to sit next to her, I struck up a conversation and quickly learnt that she was also a Reiki Master.

The medium taking the Awareness class then asked us all to stand up whilst they moved some chairs into a big circle so we could all sit facing each other (I sat next to Jules) . We were then asked to hold hands to open the circle whilst an address was made to Spirit. I recall holding Jules hand and feeling a sense of excitement.

As soon as that opening of circle had finished and we'd let go of hands the medium turned to Jules and I and said, *"are you two together?"* we replied no and she said *"well, there's a green aura around you both"*.

As we left the church, we were chatting about Reiki and I felt drawn to her and asked if she would like to meet for a coffee, to this day we laugh because she replied with a staunch *"I'm married"*, and I got the message clearly that she would not feel comfortable meeting with me, but we did stay in touch and in the early days Jules gave me a lot of guidance around the healings that I was experiencing. Some months down the line, Jules shared with me that her marriage was on the rocks and had been for a long while. It was very difficult because I had strong feelings for her, but did not want to get involved with a marriage split and I know she struggled morally with the breakdown of her relationship. Jules eventually separated from her husband and shortly after that we embarked on a relationship together.

She is absolutely amazing, so beautiful inside and out and anyone who meets her loves her.

She's been such a huge support for me over the past two years.

I have been fast tracked through this spiritual development process and there are many of the old mediumship establishment that feel it's not possible for this to happen, but Jules and indeed Debbie have been able to explain why it is so, and this gave me a huge amount of confidence.

I admire anyone who puts in the dedication for this work and has the courage and belief in Spirit to stand up and say we can heal you.

I say "we" because I never take credit for the miraculous work, the Spirit team can perform through people like us.

Jules was becoming more and more interested in mediumship and she invited me to a Wednesday night awareness course in Belfast run by a medium called Keith. There were only about six of us on the course on the first night and as soon as Keith walked into the room and sat down with us, he introduced himself and then turned to me and said *"you have amazing trance healing ability"*. I said *"I haven't got a clue what you're on about mate ? "* and at that time I honestly didn't.

The evening was interesting, but I didn't really feel drawn to it, I would go just to be with and support Jules, but the course got cancelled anyway because Keith had a bereavement in the family and had to return to Liverpool.

A day or two after the awareness evening with Keith I got a call from Sarah a young girl I had done a healing with in Carrickfergus, asking If I could give her Debbie's number because she would like a reading with her, I didn't actually have Debbie's number at that time, but I said I would go to the spiritualist church the coming Sunday and get it from her.

I was delighted to see that Debbie was actually the platform medium that evening and I watched her work with the congregation. When the evening had finished I walked up to the stage and when I got to it she said hello, and before I could say another word she said " *I've been told by Spirit I'm going to be working with you and you have trance healing* ". I was blown away.

I told her I had been told I had trance healing by another medium a couple of days ago and I didn't know what trance healing was ? She said don't worry, take my number and give me a call during the week.

I called Debbie a couple of days later and we agreed that we would meet at my apartment on the Friday afternoon at 14:00pm.

She showed me how to "sit in the power", a form of meditation but she invited the Spirit guides to join us , she would point out to me who she could see working with me from the Spirit world and also allowed Spirit to talk to me through her. This was my first experience of trance mediumship, I was fascinated and felt very privileged to have this one-on-one communication with the Spirit world.

We continued to sit every Friday at the exact same time at my apartment, and on one occasion as we arrived, she sat down on the sofa and I walked to the kitchenette to put the kettle on, as I walked back towards the lounge area, I had the most unfamiliar sensation come over me, I felt as if I wasn't my whole self, that I was huge, my skin was buzzing and my voice sounded like it was coming from inside my chest. That's the only way I can describe it. At first I felt a panic rising but she said it's ok don't worry , come and sit down, it's your Spirit guides blending with you . I would never contradict anyone's experience of Spirit blending with them, I'm sure it can depend on how an individual interprets the sensation, but I can tell you that to this day, I feel a physical energy come from behind my head and over my face. It's truly profound and again I felt incredibly privileged and humbled in fact.

I slept well that night but had very vivid dreams of my late parents. The next day when I rose out of bed, I still didn't quite feel myself, I found it difficult to focus on what I had to do, I just didn't feel present, it was an odd feeling and I called Debbie. She said I needed to ground myself.

How do I do that I asked? and she said there are a number of ways, sometimes a sea salt bath will help or walking around in bare feet or better still walking along a beach. I did all three of these exercise's to try and get back to some feeling of normality and Browns Bay was only fifteen minutes from my home.

It's a beautiful sandy beach and there's not many people there, so I decided I'd go there. I walked along the beach bare foot and paddled in the sea. When I got home I had a sea salt bath and after all that I felt much better.

Debbie and I continued to sit at my apartment every Friday from 14:00pm until 16:00pm , it's important to have discipline around this as the Spirit team will be wanting to work with us and the connection gets stronger the more reliable you are with the timing. Later on, she was told by Spirit that two other ladies would join us, forming a circle of four and these were Karen and Jacquie, both developing mediums and healers.

The love and energy generated during our Friday afternoon sessions is amazing and in the last forty- five minutes we generally take turns to give healing to each other. It's absolutely our favourite time of the week.

Connection with Spirit

I continued to meet or "sit in circle" as it's referred to by mediums each Friday, and this required one of us to open our sessions with a prayer to Spirit, during which we held hands and closed our eyes. I was taught that it was vitally important to include in the opening prayer a request for the "white light of protection ".

This is to protect you and your home from negative energies and I request this every time I sit and meditate on my own. I have had experiences where I failed to do this and the consequences were not pleasant.

I've felt uneasy indoors, anxious at night, which meant I couldn't sleep and felt a real heaviness around me. I struggled to focus on my day job. These are the negative energies that can get drawn to someone who begins this work if you are not careful. At the end of the sitting, we would thank Spirit during our closing prayer.

Debbie is also a trance speaking medium which means that Spirit guides can use her to communicate directly with people and on many occasions she would go deep into a meditation, her expression changes and she begins to speak fluently and in words that are not her own.

It's a very profound experience and I have been so privileged to have received these direct communications from Spirit guides. On Friday, September 15, 2016, Debbie and I were sat in my apartment, she went into trance and Spirit spoke to me. In not so many words, they told me why I had been chosen, and they asked for my permission to allow them to work with me, which I consented to.

I actually wrote down what was said and it reads like a contract.

More recently, I commissioned a local Carrick artist Nichole to paint the words I received that day. I invited Spirit to guide her and it's a piece of work that is my absolute pride and joy.

I still sit every single day and without fail my Spirit team make themselves present by softly and gently bringing their energy field into contact with mine.

I feel the familiar cobweb sensation of fine pins and needles from the back of my head which slowly comes around my ears and onto my cheeks. Sometimes I get a gentle pressure, like a finger pressing below my right eye socket. I continue to sit in circle each week, I have learnt so much in that time and Debbie has learnt that she has a wonderful capacity for teaching.

She told me that Spirit had informed her that what I was experiencing was new, it was a new Spirit technology and that sometimes there was a "Harry Edwards" energy working with me.

Harry Edwards was a gentleman who became one of the world's most famous spiritual healers. He was born in 1893 and died in 1976. One of nine children, his father was a printer and his mother had originally been a dress maker. As a young man, Harry entered a seven year printing apprenticeship, upon completion of this apprenticeship in 1914 he enlisted in the Royal Sussex Regiment in order to serve his country during the first world war.

He was commissioned in the field, achieving the rank of captain, and was sent to Persia (now Iran) to take charge of scores of local labourers who were tasked to build a link between two sections of the Baghdad to Mosul railway.

Injuries and illness led to many of the locals coming to him for medical treatment, despite the fact that Harry had only the barest essentials with which to treat them. Nevertheless, the recovery rate was remarkable and word soon spread of his healing powers.

Harry returned home in 1921 . He was of a Church of England background and had been rather sceptical of spiritualist claims. However, in 1936 he was led to an "open circle " (a group of mediums that sit together to develop their connection) and it caused him to reconsider his views.

He was told he had healing and was encouraged to intercede on behalf of a person dying from tuberculosis. That person subsequently made a full recovery.

His next patient was a person suffering from terminal cancer, through who, following Harry Edward's help, soon became well enough to return to work.

Many similar cases followed and, as media interest increased, Harry's reputation – and that of spiritualist healing in general- soared.

Harry went on to hold healing demonstrations at the Royal Festival Hall in front of a packed audience and founding the Harry Edwards Spiritual Healing Sanctuary, which is still going strong to this day.

Harry wrote a book, and it's a healers manual. I have a copy and refer to it often when I'm about to heal someone who has been presented to me with a specific condition or there is an outcome that took me by surprise.

It's almost as if he has been coaching me by sending me clients who have a condition that he is able to describe the prognosis and treatment of.

Shortly after that September 15 contract with Spirit I began to feel different sensations throughout my working day and on occasions during the night. I could be driving to my next insurance claim and get an unbelievable sharp stabbing pain in one of my feet or toes, it would actually cause me to swear out loud, it was that painful. It didn't last very long , but these happened quite regularly for a few months. I began to get bloated before we sat in circle or before I performed a healing, due to the energy that would build in my solar plexus.

Very vivid dreams began to occur, people who were strangers would enter my mind so clearly , I could see their features, what they were wearing , what surroundings they were in .

Sometimes these images were quite disturbing, people that looked like they had been badly burnt or injured, or I may witness a shooting. I later found out that I am a rescue medium and I will explain that in more detail a little later on in the book.

When I was healing somebody I began to feel like tiny wires of energy emitting from the finger-tips of my right hand, to begin with only my right index finger tip, but as time went on it became every finger-tip.

It's the wires of energy that people I treat feel entering and heating up or manipulating the inside of a wound, injury site or sickness area.

Harry Edwards says that the pineal gland, which is located in the base of your brain, is like a master computer that controls all cells in your body. He goes on to say that we all have intelligent and not so intelligent cells located, depending on the work they have to do .

So your organ cells, which have a big responsibility, are intelligent and your skin cells don't need to be quite so as they don't have so much to do. Sometimes, when a person experiences trauma or has a prolonged exposure to stress and or anxiety, it can knock this pineal gland " computer control centre " out of sync and that's when we get sick with conditions such as arthritis and cancer.

I have performed many healings now across a whole range of conditions, including Cancer, Crohn's Disease, Rheumatoid and Osteoarthritis , Chronic Obstructive Pulmonary Disease COPD, Diabetes, Fibromyalgia as well as less serious conditions such as sciatica and muscle strains. However, it's important to acknowledge that it is Spirit carrying out the healings, not me.

I am just a channel or medium for them to use. It's a partnership and the more you work with them, the stronger the connection gets. It's got to a level now where I'm an open medium, that is to say that Spirit guides are pretty much with me all the time and often I can sense when I'm in the company of someone, sometimes a complete stranger, who needs healing.

In many cases the recipient's not only healed physically but also experienced life changing emotional healings. I have been taught a lot by Spirit in a short period of time and all the while I have felt very guided by the Spirit team who work with me, and of course Debbie and Jules.

Not everybody will heal in the way they sometimes expect or hope for though, sometimes a person has had such a self-destructive lifestyle for so long that not only is the damage to their physical body so severe, but that even if they were to heal, they would simply continue the same lifestyle.

In all cases however, it is my opinion that there is always a form of healing that takes place, and even for those who I'm not even in the presence of. This form of healing is called distance healing and I do a lot of this as well, as it's very highly effective. I have done healings in many different environments, sometimes with complete strangers who have crossed my path, sometimes, in bars, sometimes I will visit a person at their home if they are incapacitated and many of course in my apartment surgery .

I will give some examples of these different experiences in the next chapter and hopefully in doing so I will be able to give an important insight into the incredible factual healing energies that the Spirit world is able to channel through people like me.

However, I can relate to those who cannot comprehend or fathom this healing ability that I and others have, and many more are just discovering. I don't feel that I was necessarily born with a particular spiritual ability, and having analysed all the encounters I have had with different mediums around the UK, it all points towards the fact that I may have been chosen and chosen in mid-life.

Up until the point where these spiritual happenings began to manifest with me, I had no particular beliefs, either religious or spiritual. If I couldn't see it, feel it or touch it, then I didn't buy into it or believe it.

At times the experiences I have had were at best a bit freaky and at worst, damn well petrifying, there were no rational explanations.

I include the occasion where the entity first visited me in Hertford and pinned me to the bed, and many occasions since where I have literally found myself stirring in the early hours by an energy that has absolutely vibrated my whole body from head to toe and levitated me. I have had physical encounters with "elementals", seen and heard Spirits and struggled at times to cope with the enormity of what I was discovering.

Everyone is entitled to an opinion or belief about existence, the universe, life, death, how we came to be, where we came from and what happens to us when we die. Even if someone says, "well I don't believe in anything, you die and that's it, end of ! " Well, that's a belief. My reply would be, "well, who do you know that's died, come back and told you there's nothing there ? ". I would invite you to come and meet a medium like Debbie Griffin for a reading and see if you can disown her communications from this dimension we just simply cannot see?

However, I have to say that whilst I believe in a Divine Spirit and a Spirit world that has many levels, I still wouldn't class myself as religious and I don't attend church.

I have been to Jerusalem and I visited the Church of the Nativity in Bethlehem on the West Bank. I found it interesting that this church is shared by the Greek Orthodox Church , Armenian Apostolic, Roman Catholic, Coptic Orthodox and Syriac Orthodox religions. This church is built on top of the fabled stable where Jesus was born. You enter down into its underground vaults, where its ceilings are arched and timber clad and there on the ground is a silver star.

Wow, amazing I thought, how inspiring and then when you exit this building, you realise you're in a war zone, there's shelled derelict modern offices opposite .

Religion is still the number one cause of so much violence, suffering, death and destruction in our modern day life; it's so sad and so unnecessary. I feel so privileged to be working with a new Spirit dimension that I am learning about, which has absolutely nothing but love and compassion about our planet, mother nature, the animal kingdom and of course us.

Don't get me wrong, I am still no Angel or consider myself Holier than Thou.

I love a good laugh, swear like a trooper sometimes, I enjoy a good night out, will tell someone where to go if I think they are being cheeky, but always , always, I we will respond and help or heal where I am called to do so. I feel very compelled to do this and extremely privileged to be able to do it .

Healing experiences

In this next chapter I will give you some insight into a few of the examples of healings I have experienced, and the results and the observations I made from them.

I have done many, but I'll select a few that I feel were the most profound or significant in some way. I've been shown a great deal in a short time and there have been lessons to learn from some of the people that have come into my path and their individual healing experiences.

There is always healing given from Spirit, but everyone has a free will and if it's in a person's mind-set to resist, then of course there will not be any significant physical or emotional benefit. Furthermore, if it's time for them to " go home" to Spirit because their condition is so chronic, then the healing will be to assist with this process, to ease their suffering emotionally and physically during this period. In the majority of the conditions that Spirit have treated through me, I can recognise that as well as the physical illness or pain being relieved , there has also been a healing on an emotional level. It's also important for the healer to have absolute faith and confidence in that Spirit will, heal others through them, otherwise this can block the energy.

I never have any doubt whatsoever when I perform healings in my treatment room or out in public places, that there will not be a positive result, even if they are complete random strangers and I never see or hear from the person again.

Arthritis:
Alan learned about me through the gym I attended. He had heard that my personal trainer had a bad back which I healed for him. I bumped into this gentleman in the car park outside my apartment one day, he introduced himself and asked if I would be able to assist him.

He told me he had chronic Osteoarthritis in both knees.

He was a big guy, 6ft 2inches, heavy set and apparently he was an ex body builder.

These day's he's a full time driving instructor. He explained to me that he is hardly able to walk because his knees were so painful. They were so bad, that when the hospital physio saw his x-rays , he went *"wow, they are really bad, I should be able to put a pen through those joints and you wouldn't even get a needle through them, you need new knees. "*

Prior to performing a healing I generally "sit in the power" for twenty minutes if I can, I ask for the "white light of protection" and invite Spirit doctors and surgeons to "blend with me".

If I'm made aware of a particular illness or disease prior to a client's arrival, I'll also speak with the Spirit team and invite them to heal that condition. On the evening he arrived I sat him in the big treatment chair I have, put the background music on, invited him to relax, close his eyes and told him that when I feel it's done, I'll gently touch him on the shoulder and ask him to come back slowly into the room.

The Spirit team by this time have made themselves physically known to be blending with me. I generally allow my palms to hover over the client's head for about 10 minutes, I feel this is a way that Spirit can anaesthetize a person and then I will feel the finger tips on my right hand begin to buzz and the wires of energy or fine lasers are ready to be directed into the damaged or affected area. In this case of course it was his knees. I sat on a stool next to him and these lasers were shooting into his knee joints, but I also felt that they needed to go to his left hand, which was resting on his thigh.

Most of the time my eyes are closed and I allow myself to go into a meditative state, occasionally I'll open my eyes to move around the person's body, depending on what I sense. This is what works for me and my Spirit team, and whilst there are many different healers and psychic surgeons out there with different techniques, none of them are right or wrong, it's just a personal preference.

It will get to a certain point and I will feel the Spirit team gently pull back and that's when I know they are done.

Generally this will be after about 30 – 35 minutes, but sometimes quicker. I stroked him on the shoulder and when he woke he said he could feel heat down his legs and on his hands, he was looking at his left hand , opening and closing it and I said," what is it ?" He said, " I can open and close my hand, I couldn't do that before I came to you, I have Rheumatoid arthritis in my hands and the left one was getting more and more shaped like a claw, that's amazing".

I always advise clients to drink plenty of water and that they might feel very tired later, and to just take themselves off to bed if they feel like it, regardless of what time they normally do so. Also, sometimes they will have a bit of a headache because of all of the energy that's been channelled into them, and they may have vivid dreams.

I called Alan a few days later and he said he felt amazing, had been sleeping far better than ever before and was in very little pain.

I had never treated an arthritic condition before and I was impressed at what Spirit had been able to achieve. I was drawn to my Harry Edwards book to see if he could explain how this could be.

Harry says that those in the Spirit world have far more advanced understanding of molecules and matter and how this can be changed with energies that we could simply not fathom.

He says ;

"when healing enters into the picture, movement is restored to the joint, either instantaneously or over

a period of time. In public healing demonstrations instantaneous healing of chronic arthritic conditions has often been witnessed. For this to happen, it must mean that the cementing substances have been removed.

*When healing is progressive then it indicates the substance is being changed gradually. What is certain is that a **chemical change** has been induced within the affected joint, removing arthritic deposits."*

Over the coming weeks that followed that first healing , I saw him to begin with once a week for the first four weeks and then once a fortnight for a month.

Overall the treatments lasted about two months and he was completely pain free, In fact he was able to return to the gym for the first time in years and begin light training which enabled him to lose weight.

He kindly agreed to provide a testimony on YouTube for me and he also states that he had type two diabetes which has now also healed to the point where he feels he no longer needs insulin. He has gone on to improve more and more and after nine months he is still absolutely pain free from Arthritis. As a result he persuaded his mother who had Chronic Obstructive Pulmonary Disease (COPD) and I will also provide an account of that experience in this chapter.

Spontaneous arthritic healing:
There's a lovely gentlemen who drinks in my local Weatherspoon's ("spoons"). He's a real character, and very knowledgeable about local history. He's a semi-retired civil engineer in his mid-seventies and he has to sometimes walk on crutches. He needed two knee replacements.

On this particular day I saw him sat at a table in the bar on his own, his crutches lent against the stool, and I went over and sat with him to drink my pint.

As we were chatting, I could suddenly feel the Spirit guides blending with me, and my hands began to omit energy from my palms and my right hand finger tips started to send laser like sensations to his right knee.

Now , as far as I knew, he did not know that I did healing and to be honest, I really didn't think he would entertain this, being of an engineering mind set. However, I felt compelled to ask him what's going on with your knee ? He replied that over the last few days it had become more painful than ever before.

I said to him, well look I'm a healer and at the moment you're getting healing. He said *" oh aye"*, and I sensed he was open to this. Now "spoons" can be a lively environment , but I don't let it bother me.

So he and I sat there for about twenty minutes, not speaking a word between us whilst there were punters chatting and laughing in the background, I bowed my head and let my hands hover over his knee.

It was a very powerful sensation. I could feel these wires of laser- like energy firing from my right hand finger tips into his knee joint, whilst my left hand palm was omitting energy towards him.

When I felt it was done and the Spirit team had pulled back, I said, there you go mate. He said thank you, and I left him to go to the bar for another drink.

Two days later, it was a lovely sunny evening and that's when a lot of Carrickfergus locals would go to "spoons", as it has an outside patio garden overlooking the sea and the castle.

I was standing at the bar and in he walked, I said *"alright mate, how you doing*?". I'll never forget, he just stared at me rather wryly, ordered his whiskey and ginger ale and proceeded to walk past me towards the garden door entrance. For a moment I thought I had done something to upset him and as

I watched him walk away, he held his finger in the air and shouted back "*I know you done something !!*". I laughed then as I knew the healing had worked.

He has a dry sense of humour and after about half an hour I walked out into the beer garden , said hello to a couple of friends and then he called me over to his table where he was sat with his son-in- law.

I sat down opposite him and he looked at me rather sternly over his spectacles and said these words " *now look, I'm a mechanically minded man right, and as I see it, pain is there for a reason, it's to tell me my knee's getting worse, and now you've removed my pain and I'm not sure I'm happy about it !* " I burst out laughing and said "well, I'm sorry but I can't give it back!".

I invited him to come to me for a full treatment, he said he would, but never did.

I've sat with him on a few occasions and felt the Spirit team blend with me to send him more healing and I have to say he improved further, to the point where he didn't need his crutches and even danced a few steps. He recently had his other knee replaced (the one I didn't work on) as it was booked in to be done.

Months' down the line, he says it still doesn't feel right. Interestingly, the joint of the one I treated is not sore but the ligaments on the outside of this knee are playing up and in my view this is because his "gait" has been altered, whereby his replacement knee is operating differently and therefore adding pressure to the natural knee ligaments. I often wonder what the outcome would have been if he had continued with the healing treatments instead of surgery ?

Sciatica:
On July 12 there is a huge band parade through Carrickfergus and it has to be seen to be believed, there are so many musicians, drummers, pipers and flute players it's quite a sight.

The men and women who play in these bands take tremendous pride in their involvement and some have been members pretty much all their lives from an early age, right up into their sixties and seventies still drumming and marching.

This alone can take its toll on the body, in particular the joints and spine.

I was in "spoons" one evening and there was a guy sat on a stool, I'd say he was in his late fifties or early sixties, slim build.

He looked in great discomfort as he was chatting to his friend.

I recognised the guy as we've acknowledged each other a couple of times since I'd moved to "Carrick". As I stood watching him from behind, I felt the Spirit guides blending with me and the old familiar energies began to start up from my hands and fingers, I thought "oh, here we go again". I never doubt Spirit's judgment of who, when and where they work with me, to heal others.

There's always a reason, and I always have absolute belief that the healings work. It's important to be like that because doubting yourself or the power of Spirit, as previously mentioned, can block the channels and the healing energy.

I felt compelled to offer my assistance. He told me that he was in absolute agony, he hadn't been able to work that day because his sciatica was so bad. He used to be in the army and had been a marching band drummer all his life.

I told him I was a healer and could help him 100% to get rid of the trapped nerve. He said he would do absolutely anything and so we agreed that he would come and see me the next day at 6:00pm.

Unfortunately, he didn't have a mobile so I had no way of confirming the appointment on the day, but I sat at 5:30pm and invited the Spirit guides, doctors and surgeons to blend with me to heal this man.

At 6:00pm sharp, my door buzzer went and it was him. I activated the door entry lock and told him to come up to the top floor. By the time he got to my landing I said to him I'm glad you're here mate and he said, you've got to help me please, I'm in agony.

After a very brief chat, and I had explained what was going to happen and what he might experience, I got him to climb on the treatment bed. He was wincing with pain as he tried to lay back flat but eventually he did.

After about 10 minutes, when I sensed he had settled and looked relaxed, I shifted my right hand down towards his hip, the lasers were going into this area from my right hand and after a short while, he began to contort his leg and wince. I stopped for a bit, focussing both palms over his head to settle him and then again returned to his hip and this time his thigh, again after a while he began to jolt and contort, but I stayed there until he had stopped. The treatment lasted about 40 minutes, and when I tried to gently bring him back, he was in a very deep state of rest, so I left him for a few minutes more. Eventually I called him softly back into the room and he opened his eyes.

He had no idea where he was or who I was for a moment. He looked totally bewildered.

I got him some water and he sat up, after a couple of sips I said "you ok mate, what did you sense or feel". He said he felt a tremendous bolt of energy down his leg and a sharp pain, then nothing, it's gone completely!

At that point he became a bit emotional and said to me *"thank you so much mate, nobody has ever done anything for me "*he said he saw his father's face and that his dad beat him when he was younger, and after one fight he left home at sixteen, joined the army and never returned. He never saw his father from that day and his father was now dead.

I learn things all the time from Spirit and I felt very humbled to have witnessed and been a part of that healing, not only because of the way they carried out what I call an " adjustment " or manipulation, but also for the emotional healing that will often accompany these experiences.

I bump into this man now and then and he always comes up and gives me a big hug, he looks so unburdened and hasn't been in pain like that since.

Cancer:

I was asked in the summer of 2016 to go to a lady who was battling with cancer, I didn't know what form it was, all I was told was that she was receiving chemotherapy, she was very weak, had spent months confined to her home and mainly her bed, due to pain which, as a result, caused two fractures in her lower discs.

She lived in an area of Carrickfergus, which was quite well kept, I recall the estate she lived on was well presented, with wide avenues, lots of green front lawns, and as I pulled into the estate scanning house numbers on this sunny warm day, I recall seeing a healthy looking golden labrador sat on one of these front lawns almost expectantly, and as I drew close to this dwelling, the dog got up off its hind legs and was wagging its tale with rigour. This was the address I needed to be at. The lady answered the door bell wearing a bandana scarf on her head and looking very low and weak. I would say she was in her forties and I learnt later that at that time she had put on quite a bit of weight due to her immobility.

The dog followed me into the house wagging her tail still vigorously, and I remember her saying to me that her dog never greets strangers like this, she always barks aggressively .

Following a brief chat, where I explained to her how I work and due to the fact that at that time she was in so much pain, we agreed that it would be best if she just sat in a chair rather than lay on my mobile treatment bed. As I was treating her, I was drawn to her stomach area and felt a lot of energy going there.

Following the treatment and immediately after I brought her back into the room, she said she nearly told me to stop as there was a searing pain in her stomach at the area the bowel cancer was located.

The following day I checked with her sister to see how she had been after the treatment, and she said she had been in a bad way that night, in a lot of pain and sobbing because she believed she was going to die.

I told her sister that it was common after this kind of treatment for an emotional release.

I gave her four further treatments over the course of the next two months, each time her dog would be waiting for me out on the front lawn ready to greet me. Eight months after her first treatment,

I was contacted by this lady to say that she had got the all clear and that her and her sisters' would like to take me for a steak meal.

I was delighted and couldn't wait to see her. I met them at a restaurant in Carrickfergus marina and she looked great, she'd lost a lot of weight, her hair had grown back and she had returned to work.

Twelve months later I received a text from her asking if I could help her dog . She feared she would have to have her put down later that day .

I called her and she told me that the dog had not moved from the settee for days, and was not eating or drinking any water. She said that her hind legs were badly arthritic.

I agreed to pop round later that afternoon, and sure enough this lovely golden labrador, that greeted me on the lawn of her house a year ago, was a shadow of herself. She hardly lifted her head off of the sofa in the conservatory as I walked in, she just lay there looking very pitiful.

As I sat alone with the dog, I closed my eyes, asked for the "white light of protection" and invited my guides to blend with me.

They came in strong and when I felt I was ready, I placed her blanket on the floor in front of her, and asked her to climb down on to it and she very carefully did and laid down.

I felt the energy omitting from my left palm over her head and my right hand finger tips began shooting lasers into her hind quarters . I closed my eyes and we both sat still in this way for about 15 minutes .

 I then asked her to get up and lay down facing the other way, and she did exactly this, almost as if she knew instinctively what I was doing for her. After roughly 30 minutes, I felt my guides withdrawing and I brought myself back into the room. The dog was lying peacefully with her eyes closed.

I quietly got up from the sofa and went into the lounge to speak with the owner who was quite upset. I tried to reassure her that her dog would be fine and after a brief chat, I said I would go and say goodbye to her.

We both walked to the conservatory and I called to the dog, she looked up and I beckoned her to me, she got up onto all fours slowly and walked towards me , the first steps were a little unsteady.

The owner said the dog would no longer go out of the house because the front step causes her pain when she steps down from it. I walked the dog to the front door and opened it, I went outside and called to her to follow me, she took a moment as she looked at the step and I said " *it's ok, come on* " and her owner was shocked as she stepped down onto the front lawn .

She stood in the sunshine and sniffed the air for a few moments then walked around the side of the house and *"did her business"*.

When she came back to the front door, she looked at the step and was about to lift her front paws onto it, but hesitated as she recalled this could hurt her, again I reassured her and she climbed up and into the hallway, wagging her tail.

I saw the dog on two more occasions and she improved further, although I learned recently that the vet had operated and installed some pins in her hip, but she's doing fine to this day.

Cancer :

Debbie told me about a friend of hers whose sister was terminally ill with lung cancer. She was only forty years old, had young children and had basically been sent home by the NHS to die because there was nothing more the medical profession could do for her. I offered to go and see her with

Deb. When we arrived I was met at the door by a frail looking blond lady, but she was made up with eye lashes and make- up which didn't hide the fact that she was jaundiced. She understandably looked very sick and frightened. We sat her in a chair, I plugged my iPad and speakers in and as the soft melody played, Deb's and I began to administer the healing, I could feel the wires of energy going to her chest where she had a lung drain.

Following the treatment she said she felt relaxed. I returned the next week , on this occasion Jules accompanied me . The lady answered the door and looked in far better form, she said she had been sleeping better and I thought she seemed less jaundiced than the previous week. However, the nurse was with her and we agreed to wait in the car until she had finished changing her dressings. Jules turned to me and said she didn't think she would pull through, that in her experience she felt she should already be dead. I was frustrated by Jules's observations and felt strongly at that time, that the only reason I had been brought into this lady's path was for Spirit to heal her so she would make a full recovery and that it was important not to doubt this. This was naivety on my part. What I wasn't aware of was the woman's lifestyle that had caused her sickness was such, that if she made a full recovery she would have gone straight back down the route of self-destruction.

Deb and I continued to treat the lady, sometimes both of us together or sometimes on my own, for the next six weeks, then on the 12 July 2017, I received a call from Deb to say that her friend had passed away the night before. Deb told me that I was not to feel disappointed or upset, the healing had worked for her in that it allowed her to be comfortable, free of fear and able to be with her family at home until she was ready to pass to Spirit. In fact on the day she died, she had been out shopping that afternoon, came home, had pizza with her kids and was smoking in the back garden. She had gone to bed, a bump was heard in the night and she was found dead.

Not all healings will be curative. In some cases a healer is there to assist the individual make a transition to Spirit which is a very profound and important process to be able to provide to people.

It will allow a patient to be free from the worst of the symptoms and able to be with family and friends long enough to complete any relationship issues which form part of their "life review" in the earth bound realm. When we pass to Spirit it's believed that we are met by our loved ones firstly, then our guides and a review of our life experiences is undertaken, this can often be daunting as we will get to feel and experience the effect we had on others.

We reflect on what lessons we learned and of course where we didn't learn a lesson and what karma we have yet to resolve. This is why some Spirits who pass, get stuck in the earth bound plane, for fear of this process.

Cancer :
Jules bumped into a friend recently at the hospital where she works, and learnt that her friend's husband had been admitted with terminal cancer which initially presented with the lymph nodes but has spread causing tumours in his brain. She told Jules that he had cancer three years ago but got the all clear in spite of refusing any form of medication or chemotherapy. Her husband believed that he could heal himself with holistic supplements but the cancer had now returned with a vengeance.

Jules called me and asked if I would be prepared to go and see this man in the hospital environment and give him healing. I of course agreed and on a

Tuesday at 14:00pm I arrived at the ward and met Jules and her friend. Her husband was in a private room and was expecting me. He was in his forties, shaven head and lying on top of the bed with just his shorts on. He said hello but was clearly in agony and holding his head. I told him what was about to take place and went to the side of his bed. My guides came in very strong, in fact I felt my face was quite hot.

I had already set the intent with the Spirit doctors and surgeons to disperse these cancerous cells. I had no background music, but it felt quite peaceful, and as the Spirits channelled their energies to the man's head, he began to settle and drift off. At one point about 15 minutes in, a male and female doctor entered the room, they looked at me and I gestured for them to leave, which they did. This was one occasion where I definitely sensed Harry Edwards blending with me, he came in at the end, almost as if to supervise what procedures had been carried out, the characteristic sensations I feel are unique.

I had read his chapter on cancer before I left home and he says that dispersal of these cancerous cells can occur through profuse sweating or discharges and it's necessary to drink a lot of water to assist this process.

I advised his wife of this before I left the building and said that he may feel more sore later as a result of the energy that had been channelled into him.

The next day I checked with Jules as to how he had been and she said that her friend told her he had had a terrible night and had been in severe pain.

Two days later he had checked himself out of hospital and gone home, this was on the Thursday following my first healing with him. I went and saw him at home on the Sunday. His wife had a purpose made shed in their back garden to enable her to undertake therapies such as reflexology and aromatherapy treatments with her clients. This was the perfect environment for me to work on him and so he came and lay down on their treatment bed. I always wonder when I treat cancer patients if there has been some trauma or emotional upset in their lives, as Harry Edwards identifies this can cause the pineal gland to get knocked out of sync which can lead to rogue cells forming.

During the treatment I heard him begin to cry, I continued to channel the energy from Spirit until I felt that they had finally withdrawn.

Afterwards he told me that he had felt guilty for all the burden he was causing on his family and shared about his father whom he said had been tough on him throughout his teenage years and driven him to work hard in his father's flooring business after he left school. He said he had resented his father for years because he was a hard task master but now recognised his father acted out of love so his son would be well skilled and financially secure. This was an emotional clearing that needed to take place.

I agreed to go and see him the following week again on the Sunday. Just before I left home I called his wife just to check he was ok for me to go and see him, she told me that he might be a bit groggy, because he had been up the night before watching the Champions League football final his team were competing in. She said he had been virtually pain free for the past four to five days and had been out in the garden putting up football flags.

When I arrived he was in a lot of pain with his head, which I believe was due to over exertion.

Six weeks after I first saw him in the hospital, I checked in with his wife who told me he had been out to the shopping centre the day before, and that they were looking to book a family holiday.

Again I reinforced the need for him to take things easy, and also eat little and often to build his strength up and of course continue to drink plenty of water. On the last healing visit, he looked the best I had seen him. He was walking without the "wheeled Zimma". His appetite was getting better and his pain had reduced greatly. However his condition remained terminal and although his appearance, attitude and pain reduction was evident, he eventually passed to Spirit.

Again I would classify this case as a " life Review" to enable a person to make a comfortable transition. A week after he passed I received a text from his widow saying that her husband had written a letter for me in a sealed envelope and could I provide her with my address so she could forward it to me. When I read it, I understood how much comfort and reassurance he had received from the experiences of Spirit healing energy before he passed. He acknowledged the importance of the service I provided and said he hoped to be working with me one day.

Emotional healing :
I've learned since embarking on this work that I find emotional healings particularly rewarding. The

reason for this is that I have been able to witness a profound transformation of an individual's personality or behaviour as a result of Spirit healing energy removing whatever emotional blockages they may have had.

Some of the underlying issues that I have encountered, which have caused a soul to behave in a troubled way, can be the result of traumatic experiences, such as someone losing a loved one or sibling in sudden or tragic circumstances. Sexual or physical abuse or post-traumatic stress all of which can cause a state of unrest over a long period of time that leaves the person burdened with deeply embedded sub-conscious thoughts and emotions which they are unable to find sanctuary from. This can lead them to become desperately depressed, anxious and even suicidal.

I've had a man walk directly up to me, stand in front of me with tears in his eyes and say that he needed help because he had felt compelled to cut his own throat with a "stanley knife" the night before.

He was retired from the police services, single and living a life addicted to alcohol and sex.

After the healing he was very emotional and told me he lost his younger sister who was also a police officer in a car crash many years ago. He said she should never have been in the police car giving chase to another vehicle.

The police car was hit side on by a lorry and she was killed instantly. He had been unable to cope with her loss.

I have treated him twice and over the proceeding twelve months, following the last treatment, I have witnessed what I can only describe as a transformation.

He's smiling, enjoying a healthy life, sports and fitness. We have a special connection and I get such a joy out of seeing him looking so content.

Then, there are those with conditions that I refer to as "racing brains". They have had such high levels of anxiety and restlessness which have accumulated over the years to a point where they have panic attacks. The benefits of the healing treatment from Spirit will not fully be realised for a week or so.

Only after this period of recognising that they feel more relaxed and at ease and not having experienced a panic attack, will a person settle and have confidence that they have indeed had the condition removed.

Without doubt one of the most severe cases of anxiety I have encountered was with a guy I met in Carrickfergus . Paul is in his late forties, a strong barrel chested fella. In the early days of getting to know him I was very wary because he had a reputation for having quite a volatile temper and always appeared on edge to me.

However, I have witnessed a profound change in him since he eventually came to me for healing, which was no easy achievement for this tough guy, I can tell you. Eventually it took an elbow injury he sustained in the gym, which the doctors and physios couldn't assist him with, for him to ultimately give me a go.

A week or so prior to the healing treatment, both Jules and I noticed that he was not looking good. He looked very uneasy and distracted, sweating profusely in company, like he was struggling to cope with socialising.

At the time, I was not aware that he was having panic attacks.

I learned he joined the Royal Ulster Constabulary aged twenty and left in his thirties to work in personal protection.

He has looked after President Bill Clinton, Sharon Osbourne , Simon Cowell and even Royalty such as Prince Charles.

But where he really made a name for himself was protecting Reuters news crew's filming sometimes in deadly war zones such as Iraq and Syria or plane crashes such as the Malaysian one on the 17 July 2014 which was shot down over the Ukraine. Paul was one of the first on the crash scene with the news crew and the sights he witnessed were horrific.

I have read the report he had to type up for his employers on the 18th of July and it is truly harrowing. In it he records the pungent smell of burnt flesh mixed with aviation fuel, streams of blood and oil over the ground which he said he slipped on.

A decapitated body still strapped into the flight chair, burnt and severed parts of men, women and children strewn all over the fields where the fuselage broke up. He told me he felt so shocked and saddened that he said a prayer for the dead.

In 2012 he was with the Reuters news crews in Syria and nearly got captured by Assad forces.

Paul and the news crew evaded capture and certain death by hiding in a sunflower field until the troops gave up their search.

And finally In 2016 I received a WhatsApp image from him showing a vehicle that he had been travelling in which got hit by an ISIS rocket drone.

He sustained a shrapnel injury to one of his ankles and when he returned home to Carrickfergus he made the decision to not continue in that line of work.

When you consider and reflect on the incredible stress levels coupled with post traumatic stress and adrenalin fuelled " fight or flight" circumstances he had been exposed to over the years, it is no wonder it ultimately affected his ability to interact or cope with civilian life back home. The healing he received from the one session he had with me removed his anxiety and he is now far more relaxed and at ease. Furthermore, twelve months down the line and he tells me he still has not had any more panic attacks.

Chronic obstructive pulmonary disease (COPD) : In December 2017, I received a text from Alan, the guy I had treated for arthritis nine months previous. He said he was very worried about his mother Maureen . She was 81 and had been diagnosed with COPD 4 years ago. She had deteriorated badly, was housebound and had basically just given up the fight.

I called him and he told me that although she did not believe in spiritual healing, she had seen the incredible improvement that Alan had benefited from, and was therefore willing to give me a try.

I didn't know very much about the condition other than that it effects the lungs and breathing ability by over production of phlegm or mucus. It's an awful condition which is progressive and incurable. Eventually resulting in everyday activities such as walking or getting dressed becoming difficult.

I referenced Harry Edwards book to see if he had any advice on what to look for or focus on when treating this condition, but in his day, it hadn't been diagnosed or discovered. The nearest reference I could find was asthma, so I really didn't know what to expect when I went along to see her.

Maureen was laid back in a large leather electric reclining chair, oxygen mask next to her on a coffee table. She looked very frail with dark rings around her eyes where she hadn't been sleeping much, her back and neck were sore as a result of her poor posture and she was coughing a lot of mucus up.

Alan and I managed to get her out of the big reclining chair and into a more upright position where I could work on her. Alan left the room , I put my background music iPad on and Spirit blended with me . During the treatment I felt wires of energy going to her neck, back and of course I brought my right hand around to the chest area to focus healing to her lungs.

Whilst she coughed a few times, she did settle and we managed to complete a full 30 minutes. Afterwards, I asked how she felt and she said it was an amazing feeling, she could feel heat in the areas that I knew the Spirit doctors and surgeons had been working on.

I left it a couple of days and then checked in with Alan to see how she was and he said he had noticed a marked improvement, she wasn't coughing so much, her back and neck pain had gone and she had actually managed to sleep in her bed instead of the leather reclining chair.

I saw Maureen every week for six weeks and the improvements were incredible. She felt well enough to do her own washing, make the bed, clean her kitchen cupboards, and she wanted to leave the house. However, It was bitterly cold weather at that time so I advised she waited until it was warmer and bless her, she did.

I first saw Maureen in December 2017 and I made a surprise visit to her home in July 2018. I was in her living room when she returned home from a short shopping trip. She looked amazing, no more coughing and was so happy to have been given a new lease of life. I felt very humbled and privileged to have been able to facilitate this for her.

Distance Healing :

Distance healing is a very potent form of healing. It is not performed in the presence of a patient, there is no contact and often the healer would not even know the recipient. Devine or Spirit healing is common to all religions and has been for thousands of years. It is a universal law that requires a directive or request to be given to the Spirit guides before any healing can take place. In religious circles it can take the form of prayer and with a spiritual healer it's through attunement during meditation. Harry Edwards healing sanctuary received literally thousands of letters a week requesting healing, a testimony to the efficacy of this phenomena.

Sometimes the results can be immediate and sometimes they improve over a period of time.

I found that I prefer to use my healing book. It is very special to me and I take it on my travels. Its leather bound with a strap and I write the names of those which I wish to send distance healing to and or the condition I wish Spirit to heal or assist with. On some occasions it can be situations that I ask Spirit to intervene with that I've read about or seen in the news which can be anywhere in the world. I will then sit in meditation and hold it between both palms and feel the energy from my hands go into it.

The results are incredible, on occasions I have listened to a friend tell me about a relative that's suffering and without telling them, I will write the name in the healing book and ask Spirit to aid that individual. The next time I see that friend I will ask how their relative is doing and always without fail, there has been a marked improvement. I get requests from mediums, including the head of the Hertford Spiritualist church, Debbie West. From time to time and they will give me feedback and it's always very positive.

There are two examples I think demonstrate the power of distance really well .

The first is with Dean, yes Dean the accident prone who lived in 3 Temple Gardens with my brother and I all those years ago. In Oct 2017, I flew with Jules to London, it's the first time she had been there and she wanted to visit all the places from my upbringing and meet with my boys Luke and Kane and others I grew up with. I had recently reconnected with a few friends from my past that I'd lost touch with including Dean, who I hadn't spoken to for seven years.

I learnt Dean had spent the past five years of his life trying to "pass the knowledge "and become a black cab taxi driver of the City of London. I recall seeing many guys on mopeds driving through the streets of London with clip boards stuck to the handlebars as they traced routes and tried to absorb these and all the thousands of street names and building locations in their memory so they could recount these journeys in front of the London Black cab board of examiners. There are literally thousands of random routes these examiners can call on an examinee to trace during their test and it's a lot of pressure. Why Dean decided the best way to do this was on a peddle bike, is still beyond me? But that's the mode of transportation he decided upon and as you can imagine, it was going to take a considerably longer time to achieve than speeding around on a moped. Ultimately, he had failed the exam twice and his pure level of gut determination meant he was never going to give up the cause.

On the Friday night Jules and I arrived in London, we met Dean in the Queens Head pub Winchmore Hill . He was looking quite downtrodden, there was no bounce or positivity in his energy.

He was stiff and in pain - the consequences of his many physical injuries had taken their toll on his fifty three year old body, in particular his ankles, which he broke six years earlier drunk on vodka with his mum Stella. They were both in her back garden drinking, when the neighbour's kids lost their football over the allotment fence at the bottom of the gardens. Dean leapt over the fence to retrieve the ball, but when he returned, for some unknown reason he stood upright on top of the fence post and when he dropped off, he didn't bend his knees, and upon landing on the hard ground instantly shattered his ankles, which is commonly known as a "lovers break" eluding to the fact that this happens to many a man who leapt out of a bedroom window to evade capture.

We had a lovely evening, Jules had Dean up dancing to the DJ, but we left early to go to meet my son Kane in his home town. The next morning I received a call from Dean at 8:00am , he sounded very groggy and confused as he asked me *"how did I end up in hospital?"*. I said I don't know mate, what happened ? He didn't know how he had sustained injuries to his head, his body was all bruised but he recalls riding home on his peddle bike and that was the last thing he remembers.

Dean sustained severe concussion, and in the subsequent weeks after his discharge from hospital, severe depression and panic attacks.

He was completely emotionally disabled from work and lived in isolation in his flat and the consultant told him this could last for weeks, months or indefinitely.

We were all deeply concerned for him, and although I had to return home to Carrickfergus that following Sunday, I called Dean every morning and every night in the days that followed to check in on him.

When I got home I wrote Dean into my healing book for his brain injury, panic attacks and depression to be healed.

Within a very short space of time I could tell when I spoke to him over the phone that emotionally he was improving, his anxiety attacks had ceased. Although he wasn't quite out of the woods and it did take weeks, eventually he wasn't feeling depressed either, but I noticed he began to go through what I would again label as a kind of "life review". This can happen to someone who has been stuck in a rut for a long time, unable to see a positive way out of a situation or lifestyle. Sometimes it will take something major to disrupt this hopeless and unfulfilling path, such as an injury, loss of a loved one or serious illness, for the person to pause and take stock of their life.

When we spoke, Dean would be questioning why he was still stuck with the black cab taxi course, and always short of money.

I requested Spirit intervention for him, to guide him in a more rewarding career path.

I really wanted to give him a direct healing treatment and as he began to feel much better, relieved that his depression had left, I offered to fly him over for a weekend visit to stay with me in my apartment. It was a wonderful opportunity to explain to him about the healing that I did and the amazing discoveries I had made about the Spirit world. Before he flew home he agreed to let me treat him. I called him the next day to see how he was, he told me his knees and ankles were not as sore and over the coming days and weeks he continued to improve. With his new found agility he began to consider a career change and dropped the black cab taxi course to embark on a decorating venture. He was always a good decorator but his knees and ankles restricted his ability to work every day. I was delighted, and every week since he returned home I've kept in touch to see how he is doing. Eight months after he sustained the head injury he has a good sustainable income from his decorating business, making good money again and looking to buy a new van and I am delighted for him.

The next example relates to a couple that emigrated to Australia from Winchmore Hill, North London twenty years ago and whom I recently reconnected with.

John is a builder and Alison is a nurse, both in their late fifties.

They have two children, a son that lives with them and a daughter who lives in England.

The daughter has two children, the youngest of which is three and suffers from severe asthma and was being hospitalised on average twice a month due to severe attacks.

Once a year Alison flies to England to visit with her daughter and grandchildren for a month.

On the 15th of May I received a text from Alison to ask if I could send her granddaughter distance healing and of course I did. Six months later and she hasn't had another attack.

The child also suffers from severe eczema. With the exception of some infectious disease, the origin of eczema lies in some form of nervous or emotional stress, and therefore this unbalance must first be rectified before the skin will clear.

I have every confidence that in the months that follow, and as the child begins to recognise that her asthma attacks have ceased, she will relax more and her eczema will also improve.

Developing with Spirit

There is much we don't know about the other dimensions. Scientists are researching dark matter and exploring space for answers. I believe that my guides present information to me as their teachings require. This information can take many forms, sometimes I'm drawn to research the internet, or they will channel vocal messages through Debbie direct or I will experience something in my dream state that will prompt me to investigate its meaning.

Since discovering I have the ability to heal others, I have been dedicated to developing this connection with Spirit guides. I sit in the power every morning and sometimes in the afternoon. The length of time generally varies depending on my work commitments but in the early days I would sit for 45 minutes to an hour. Prior to this I would speak openly to my guides and ask for the white light of protection , then invite them to draw close to me to assist me to go deep into the stillness where they can prepare me to be a clear channel for their healing energies and I would ask that their healing energies be sent to all those people and situations in my healing book, and I would ask this in accordance with the divine plan and 100% for the greater good amen.

If someone wishes to embark on this work to develop a psychic ability I would always advise that this is done initially either in a circle, possibly at a spiritualist church or through a Reiki program. There you will receive guidance and the necessary attunement's from the mediums.

It takes a lot of patience and dedication, even though in some spiritual circles I'm still regarded as a bit of a rookie, I have been fortunate enough to have had very good foundation attunement's through the Reiki Mastership program and then the development that Debbie dedicated herself to in our closed circles with Karen and Jacquie.

I would also add that it's important to be bold enough to actually carry out healing work on others, especially in the early days, otherwise there would be little point in your guides dedicating their time to your cause. They will expect punctuality and reliability. Even if one or either of us can't make our Friday sitting, the remaining who are available will. On occasions it's been just two or three of us, but we will still sit. Invariably it will still be a rewarding experience.

Spirit communicate with us in many ways, verbally through mediums such as Debbie, intuitively by placing thoughts or feelings in our mind or through our dream state and in my experience usually between the hours of 3:00am and 5:30am is when most Spirit activity takes place. I have had incredible and quite frankly, hard to believe experiences around that time.

On one such night, in the early hours, I had a physical encounter with two Elementals " Billy and Enoch", I was conscious and not in a dream state. Jules had given me an array of crystal's some time ago and I have them laid out on a low partition wall which is capped off with a wooden shelf between my kitchenette area and my lounge which is directly below my galleried bedroom .

Quite frequently I would hear a tap in the night, like one of the stones had been lifted and set down hard on the wooden shelf. This would be followed by a sense that there were Spirit's in my apartment and I would either have vivid images of people enter my mind as I slept, or I would have this overwhelming vibrating energy from head to foot which would cause me to have an out of body experience. In the early days when this happened, I was conscious, but I couldn't open my eyes or call out. More recently as I have become more accustomed to this amazing sensation, I feel relaxed and to be honest quite excited as to what might follow. I think this is why I have been allowed to sometimes open my eyes if I wish and I have witnessed some incredible sights.

However, on the night in question, it was a very hairy experience and I recall it vividly.

I was not late to bed, around 11:30pm, and was in a relaxed sleep state when I heard the tap of the stone twice. Then the energy began to vibrate me from head to foot as I lay on my back and I felt as if I was being sucked out through the top of my head like they were trying to transport me somewhere. I tried to open my eyes but couldn't, so I consciously decided to go with it. I'm not exactly sure how long it lasted for, maybe 15-20 minutes and then it came to a halt. It was deathly silent and I was still laying on my back and just about to open my eyes, when I felt someone gently massaging my toes on each foot, almost like reflexology, it felt nice and I don't know what prompted me to say this, but I said out loud *"hello, who are you? I'm Will "* in the politest matter of fact way I could, so as not to startle them.

My eyes were still closed and I then heard a gravelly, slightly high pitched voice say *"Billy"* and his second name which I can't remember and then another voice in a similar tone say *"Enoch"* and his second name. I recall feeling shocked but realising I needed to keep my nerve and I wanted to try and remember everything that was said, I felt the urge to open my eyes and see who they were, but was afraid they might startle and disappear, so instead I held out my right hand off the edge of the bed and said *"pleased to meet you ? "* In turn they took my hand and held it for a second. Their form felt like dense energy as opposed to solid matter like ourselves. It was an incredible sensation. I asked them why they were here and they said I was not well, that there were too many mediums working with me and that they were tweaking me, at that point I felt energy going into my stomach. Then Billy, who I could establish had been working on my feet, climbed up on the bed next to me on my left side. I could feel his weight and movement on my duvet cover. He asked if I liked Halloween, in a rather child-like innocent manner, and so as not to offend, I replied yes I do. He then asked if I could draw him a witch and I replied yes but you'll need to get the paper from the printer downstairs in the kitchen and a pen.

At that point I heard a distant voice, the kind you might hear if someone took a phone call who was nearby, you could hear the sound of someone's voice but not what was being said, but I got the sense that it was a man, and that he was not happy with these two making contact with me.

Moments later I sensed they had left. I opened my eyes sat up, looked around and recall saying what the fuck had just happened here !!

I went downstairs, got a glass of water and went back to bed, eventually getting back off to sleep.

The next day I was really struggling to come to terms with the experience. I had encountered and met with beings from another realm, it was profound and very unsettling and I doubted anyone would believe me.

I rang Jules and told her, she said she believed they were mischievous elementals who had come through a portal to maybe undertake the practical adjustments and any repair work on behalf of the Spirit world and that they were in trouble for breaking a code of anonymity which was why a call came into them probably from a higher being of authority and they left.

She told me about a special medium called Brian Lynch who gives spiritual assessments and I should call him for advice so I took his number and called him later that day after work. I didn't expect him to answer the phone as I understood he is booked out many months ahead with many readings and medium assessments, but he did answer and I was able to impart what happened the night before and also tell him about all the vivid images I was seeing before I woke. Brian could tell I was very distressed. He suggested I come and see him soon and that although he was very booked up for months , he would try and get me squeezed in and eventually two weeks later I got to meet him at his home in a fashionable part of Belfast. Brian's a well-kept man in his fifties with long parted grey hair, a softly spoken and reassuring gentleman who has developed a gift for mediums like myself to go and have a meeting with him and your Spirit guides. It's an incredible feeling of being so close with your guides, as he begins to tell you what they say is happening around your spiritual development. I have it taped and Jules and I listened to it whilst I was writing this book. He told me that I have a concrete connection with my guides, that primarily I have a very strong healing ability with them but other gifts will unfold in time.

So much has come true and during the session he asked me if there was anything I'd like to ask my guides, so I asked them why was I seeing vivid people in my mind's eye and feel that I am in situations with them.

He responded by telling me that whilst I was a healer, I was also a rescue medium and that this is a specialist field of mediumship that he is familiar with, because he is also one. It means that I have been travelling to Spirit planes to be with those who have passed to Spirit world but that got stuck in the lower planes . Apparently there are many in each level of lower, middle or higher category and that to begin with I will be working In lower planes which he acknowledged sometimes isn't a very pleasant experience, and the next morning it can make you feel a bit low, all of which I could accept and relate to.

He did say that as time goes on I will start to move to the higher planes which are far nicer. Again I know I have been there and I'll tell you more about these in the next chapter. I have learnt that some Spirits can get trapped and that they need help to go home to the light. Some mediums in the earthly plane can assist them to do this through a conscious process or in the way in which I have been utilised.

Since the episode with Billy and Enoch I researched what I could about these Elementals and pieced the pieces together with my own encounter to try and get some logic around it.

My opinion is that these are small beings which are attracted to nature. They exist at a higher vibration (a different plane) which is why we cannot see or hear them unless we are some form of medium. They are clearly childlike in personality, innocent but mischievous and get themselves into trouble.

I feel they are stubborn in nature but with good intention. I do not believe they would harm us or resent us unless we were uncaring to Mother Nature and even then, it would just result in indifference, no violence or physical haunting. Moreover they are likely to be caretakers running around trying to hold the world together and even counter the awful toxicity we cause. I also believe they are controlled or disciplined by Angels or Ascended Masters.

However, I am saddened to say that Billy and Enoch have not returned since that night, but I would very much like to engage with them again.

Multi-Dimensional work

This is the ability Spirit gave me to visit the other dimensions. This is not something I can do at will, they decide when and where this will occur and I'm not sure if this will change later down the line as they further develop me.

As I have already mentioned there are many dimension's and I believe that whilst Spirits are able to visit us in our dream state, when we meditate or communicate and show themselves to us through mediums, they are of a much higher vibration than ourselves, and so to actually visit their dimension on whatever plane that maybe, it makes sense that we would have to raise our own vibration to a level that matches theirs. This can then allow one to see their environment, touch and actually, in some cases smell it.

I have mentioned earlier in these chapters about the energy that visits me and separates my

Spirit from my physical body, this happens quite regularly now and I have been able to remain conscious to a point where they have allowed me see what is happening.

Jules was staying with me at my apartment one night, when in the early hours the energy came over me, I was firstly gently turned over from lying on my side to my back and began vibrating at a high frequency. I felt my soul lift up and float around the balconied bedroom, I squinted my eyes open and saw a grid of green lasers, there where larger round circles on each corner, again formed out of these bright green lasers, and then I saw an amazing site of three beings standing behind a kind of podium, two male and one female similar in looks, almond shaped eyes and they were blue in colour. I closed my eyes again as I felt I didn't want to upset them in any way and just allowed myself to be floated around the room, eventually settling back down into my physical body. The vibrating eventually ceased and I turned to Jules who was asleep and said " *did you see what just happened ?*", the frustrating thing was, she hadn't seen anything, in fact she was in a very deep sleep. This can be because she was used as a kind of battery, an energy boost to assist with what

Spirit were doing with me. However, I described to her as much detail as I could recall .

The next day Jules text me a picture with a short message saying "is this what you saw ?" I was taken aback as it was precisely what I saw. The formation of lasers was a Merkaba and the three beings were Arcturians.

A Merkaba is a sacred geometric structure and is believed to provide a vehicle of light that enables a soul to travel to other dimensions, and there is an image of it on the front cover of this book.

It is widely accepted that aliens exist and I have no doubt that it won't be very long before world leaders finally disclose the facts about this. American politicians refer to the next "disclosure president" and "kicking the can down the line" meaning when it comes out the US government would be impeachable for withholding the existence of aliens from the American people and so the President is reluctant to disclose during his office.

The Arcturians are believed to be one of the most advanced alien civilizations in the galaxy.

It was Edgar Cayce, the most renowned psychic of the 20th Century, also known as the "sleeping prophet" for his accurate psychic "readings" of the afterlife who communicated with the Arcturians telepathically. Cayce was bestowed with precious knowledge about their origins, nature, goals and ideology, which he further shared with the rest of the world. These masters of the galaxy are the most evolved life-form around, having ascended to the 5th dimension due to their spiritual advancement. They are the healers of the galaxy and protect mankind from other harmful extra-terrestrials.

They are preparing us for the shift into the 4th dimension which will come as a result of spiritual development. I believe that the vibration I experience is necessary to allow my soul to travel to the other dimensions and interact with Spirit people.

I recall returning back to my room following one such episode and being so humbled and grateful for what had taken place in those early hours that I was actually sobbing with joy.

Debbie and I had travelled to Hertford, England together for her to be the guest platform medium at Hertford Spiritual Church. I had stayed in touch with Debbie West the chairlady when I moved to Northern Ireland and upon my recommendation she kindly agreed to let Deb's do the Sunday ceremony. Deb's put in an incredible performance and brought through so many Spirit's with messages for loved ones in the congregation . We stayed in different hotels which were nearby and in the early hours of the Monday morning (the day we were due to fly back to Belfast) I had that familiar buzzing energy visit me, this time it drew my spirit up out of my body and suspended me high. I then saw a circular funnel of energy which I felt I was given a decision to enter and I did, in a moment I was staring out of an entrance looking down into a lush and colourful land. There was a path lined with tall palms and beyond I could make out sands and the sea, I travelled along the path and it felt I was floating, I didn't sense I had legs. I drew close to a large hut on my right which resembled a thatched restaurant of two halves, in the centre was a small reception and a tall attractive brunette woman in her thirties met me, she smiled and said *" they are in there waiting for you "*, I entered the room and saw my father, mother, uncle Derek and a gathering of other spirit people who looked like they were having fun and laughing.

I walked up to my father and we hugged, I could feel him and smell him, I held him tight and said *"it's so lovely to see you"*, then I hugged my mother and just felt such love and joy. When I hugged Derek he invited me to take a walk with him and we walked back along the path past the restaurant building on my left and the trees and beach to my right, as we travelled along for about what seemed like five hundred yards or so I could see we were coming to a group of buildings like a small town and there were many Spirit people of different descriptions. On my right there were bars and again there were Spirit people sat drinking and laughing. I felt like I wanted to stay in the land, but as we began to walk back towards the thatched restaurant, Derek stopped and we were joined by a small black gentleman who gave me a key. Moments later I was back in my hotel room lying on my back. I sat up and was just in awe of what had just happened, I felt so honoured and grateful to have had a moment with my parents and family in Spirit that I just started to sob for a while and kept saying " *Wow!*" out loud.

It's not the first time that I have been given keys when I've visited the Spirit world and I believe these may be keys to those dimensions for me to enter.

I've mentioned rescue work and this is something I have only begun to understand more recently.

In most cases I would say these are quite grey or bland experiences I have where I have met with a group of Spirits going about their daily lives, with normal activities, but on occasion they have been quite gruesome and even violent like the one where I witnessed a young man in his late twenties shoot his girlfriend.

He was a good looking young man with shoulder length brown wavy hair. He was wearing a green shirt with lapels. Across from him was this attractive blonde girl of around the same age, she had a pony tail and was taunting him saying she had slept with another because he was useless. Suddenly he pulled out a gun and shot her in the chest. She had a look of total shock and was begging for him to spare her life. The man had a look of determination on his face, as he walked up to her, grabbed her pony tail, lifted it high and shot her in the side of the head. At that point he looked directly at me with an expression of desperation and horror.

Although I did not witness it, I suspect he took his own life at that time. I feel that these souls had been stuck in that horrific event and needed awakening in order to move on.

So why do Spirits need rescuing? I believe there can be many reasons why a person's soul is unable or unwilling to enter the Spirit world. It could be because the Spirit was so fearful at the time of their death, because death itself is something they believe is the end, that there is no afterlife or they fear judgement upon their crossing for those that have committed bad or violent acts. In some case it can be that these Spirits are desperate to hold onto their physical possessions. They have spent their earthbound life building and accumulating material things which they value highly and so wish to stay attached to them. Love is another reason; these Spirits can have such an overwhelming devotion to a partner or loved ones they leave behind that they turn their back on the light that is the entrance to Spirit world.

One of the common situations I would find myself in would be with the Spirit's who believe they are in a dream. When a soul leaves their physical body their soul or Spirit resides in a non-physical form and because time no longer continues in the same way it does in an earthbound state, this can cause the Spirit to get trapped by their own consciousness, believing that they are dreaming.

These Spirits are confused and usually play out some part of their life before they died. To Spirit these seem like these events have just happened but in the earthbound plane they are being played out over and over again.

These can be regarded as hauntings. Spirits in this dream like state require a rescue medium from the earth bound plane to join them in whatever the dream like situation it is that they are focussing on, and enable the Spirit to eventually recognise that they have died to enable them to then make the connection with their guides and loved ones.

However, sometimes these lost Spirits can become aggravated or upset by this earthbound Spirit presence which can provoke them into violence.

Recently I was taken to the lower planes. The buzzing energy came upon me again and I was then away. There were two separate scenes and experiences with Spirit, but what was interesting was that after the first two, I opened my eyes, I didn't feel I wanted a long night because I had a busy day ahead. The buzzing instantaneously stopped and I said sternly aloud *"ok, that's enough"*, I then heard a male voice say clearly *" one more for the worldliness"*, and as I closed my eyes again, the vibration started immediately. I then found myself with a large overweight man, bald head and a bulbous nose, he stank of body odour and he attacked me, we wrestled and I recall pinning my hands under his shoulders to hold him at bay.

Eventually he stopped and I opened my eyes, my bedroom absolutely stank of his body odour, it was not pleasant and I got up and went downstairs to make a cup of tea.

It's not often that I hear voices from Spirit, but I do feel it's important to note them for what you hear said, as opposed to changing the words so they make more sense to you. I've googled the word *"worldliness"* and the first definition I found said *"concern with material values or ordinary life rather than a spiritual existence."*

I don't know why Spirit chose me to work in this way, I feel it's an honour and a privilege but at times it's definitely not for the faint hearted.

Raising of our Vibration

We hear many people talk of "raising their vibration" how amazing their life feels as a result, and much advice is offered as to how we can all achieve this. But what does it mean to raise our vibration?

Well, firstly it's a scientific fact that the earth has a vibration, a pulse. This was discovered in 1950 by professor Winifred Schumann who was a mathematician.

He calculated that the planet had a global electromagnetic resonance, measured in kilohertz (kHz) between its surface and the ionosphere (the Earth's upper atmosphere) which could be excited by the millions of daily lightening strikes upon the earth.

It has also long been suspected that human consciousness can impact on the magnetic field, through different variants of global anxiety, tension, passion .

On 1/31/2017 for the first time in recorded history, the Schumann frequencies reached a resonance of +36. In 2014 it was thought remarkable that it had risen from its usual 7.83 to between +15 and +25, so something very big is happening to the Earth itself. Its vibration or pulse is increasing.

Furthermore, scientists report that the Earth's magnetic field, which can affect The Schumman Resonance, has been weakening over the past 2000 years and many today feel that time is speeding up as a result of this process.

There are those that believe the Earth's magnetic field blocks our primordial, primeval or elemental heritage which was necessary for souls to learn from the experience of free will, so in effect, if the magnetic field is weakening then possibly "the blinkers are coming off ".

Perhaps this is why so many around the world are awakening at this time, and is this why many of us hear the high pitched resonance we call tinnitus ?

I believe that the Spirit realm are revealing themselves to us more and more, that they are coming closer to assist mankind and as the Earth ascends we will receive new gifts such as a globally acknowledged ability to heal ourselves.

However, not everyone will align to this as there will be those who are too stuck in their ingrained beliefs that, we are all just born a product of our planet's evolution.

That we go to school, learn an education, get a job, find a wife, buy a house, have kids, get a nice car, have a few holidays, grow old, acquire grandchildren then die , then you're put in a box in the ground and that's it . This is what I refer to as a 'three dimensional life', and I have to admit that there were times in my own life when I bought into that false belief.

Although I'm generalising here, I'm sure you get the picture that many in this world do not get to experience the true joys of realising we are magnificent spiritual beings, having an earthly experience and the full power of who we really are, what we are capable of ,how we can manifest such a beautiful way of life in this dimension, and that we will ascend to other dimensions when we leave this one.

I have learnt that as I began to embark on being open to the Spirit world and embracing the knowledge and experiences that come with it, I would intuitively feel awkward around others who are locked in their 'three dimensional life'.

Often these people were very materialistic, appeared unfulfilled and upset with their lot. I sensed they resented those who live life on a different level or higher vibration, even if they didn't understand what that was.

I believe that when we acknowledge the Spirit world, they get excited, I have physically felt this in the very early stages of them blending with me. My heart would palpitate and I find this very endearing. They are very loyal to our cause, and look after me in many ways to ensure I am unburdened as much as possible to be able to continue developing this work.

As I have said, I sit in the power every day and "call them in" and on occasion I ask for specific assistance for myself. If I have a particularly challenging day ahead ,perhaps there is a journey I have to undertake or my day job has a difficult situation to address, I will ask for their assistance and guidance . It took me a while to recognise how incredibly supportive they are to me, but they always without fail, influence things for my "greater good".

What do I mean by "my greater good ? ". Well,

I trust in their judgment on that one, because only they know what is best for me at any given time.

There were things that I desired but in-spite of requesting, never materialised, and it's only when I reflect later down the line that I can appreciate there was a very good reason for this and usually because they had something greater in line for me, or as is sometimes the case I realised it would have done me no good.

Sometimes we try and force things, instead of allowing the necessary experiences we actually require in this life to unfold, and advance ourselves emotionally, spiritually and physically.

We can get stuck at times, too focussed on "the now" and the overwhelming desires we have for situations to be as we want them to be. Just because we think and want them so badly in this or that way, does not mean they will necessarily materialise to us for our greater good at that time, if at all.

Frustration is a state of transition and it's up to us how long we stagnate at that station. To be able to manifest our true potential and incremental fulfilment in this material life, we have to sometimes stand back, take a breath and reflect from where we have come from, to fully appreciate and even get a possible sense of excitement for what might be coming down the line for us.

We are all familiar with the "Law of Attraction"; like attracts like, and I find that I am attracted to, and indeed attract to me, people that are positive, caring, fun or perhaps a bit eccentric.

Those that have triumphed through adversity as well as those that I meet who are going through difficult times. With the latter I can empathise with these people and feel compelled to offer support and healing.

When you can experience making a difference to others and having a positive impact on the community, you feel a strong sense of self-worth, love and respect for each other.

As I became more and more aware of the Spirit guides working with me, the serendipity, fate or destiny that began to unfold around me gave me a tremendous sense of separation from the old 'three dimensional' lifestyle.

I was becoming more present in the now and not being anchored to past history or events, and although there are occasions when I could get drawn back into life dramas by others, I still sensed this was a purging of my past in some way.

I believe this will end when I am able to be in the present constantly.

As many of us make this transition or ascension, we will be more aware of greater serendipity and more synchronicity. We will trust in our intuition which will take care of our progression. It will be a heart sensed path, one that will not cause concerns or fear of decisions because we will trust in our higher self to steer us with support from our Spirit guides.

In other words, we will not worry or obsess about things, we will simply go with the flow. There is a large wave of people around the planet that are moving into this new dynamic state of being, a merging of mind, body and soul. I feel comforted and reassured that there is much more to mankind than just existing to learn karmic lessons. I became more positive and excited about the opportunities and experiences that our lives could offer us. There have been many occasions where I have felt a moment of pure rapture, and this could be out in nature, taking in breath, taking in scenery or in a bar where the music and atmosphere is so positive and fun, that it's simply infectious for those I saw just entering the scene.

The more you call on your Spirit guides for assistance in lifting any moments of gloom, the less that dullness lasts. You don't have to be sitting in meditation to do this either. It can be out in public somewhere and you feel upset or anxious about a situation. Just call on them for assistance and guidance. Eventually you find that the large majority of the time, you feel a sense of gratitude, reassurance and serenity. This is what I feel best describes " living on a higher vibration " .

The End Game

I feel very passionate about the need for mankind to awaken and recognise that there are other dimensions, Spirit people and multidimensional beings that are willing to aid us. To assist with healing not just us, but the planet, the animal kingdom and mother nature. This has been a taboo subject in many professional sectors for too long. Although there are countries and health trusts that are beginning to recognise the value of alternative therapies, these are mainly for stress relief and emotional wellbeing. I stand for a lot more. I know from my own experiences that many illnesses and serious disease can be healed significantly and that those in palliative or terminal care can be assisted in the life review stages to ease their crossing over and ensure that whilst they are still in the earth bound plane, their fear and anxiety can be alleviated.

I am not advocating spiritual healing as an alternative to the medical profession, far from it. I believe that it should run concurrently as a complementary therapy. We are currently living in a society with an aging population and more chronic and long term health conditions.

I believe that the provision of spiritual healing would assist in alleviating the current pressure on acute and primary care services.

Many patients would either not require admission if treated in the early diagnostic stages, or symptoms could be significantly reduced for those in palliative or terminally ill patients.

I have seen the enormous benefit for those terminally ill patients who have received healing at the time of transition to Spirit. This has not only reduced the symptoms and emotional trauma for the patient but also their family and carers.

My vision is to have a healing centre where we can provide a foundation diploma course in spiritual healing and to provide qualified healers to the National Health Service. For these healers to be recognised as valued professionals and remunerated as such, therefore providing career opportunities.

The healing centre would also provide healing surgeries utilising our trained staff.

I hope that my journal inspires others to awaken and discover the benefits of connecting to the Spirit realm. Everything I have written in these pages is a true account of the encounters, events and experiences I have had, some of which seem unbelievable and I have tried to explain this as much as I can, but I certainly don't profess to know all the answers.

I am still unfolding, and whilst I do not know what the future holds, I will stay true to the cause and promote the relationship mankind can have with the amazing Spirit realm until I return home there myself.

Love and light to you all.
Will

Reading References

Harry Edwards : A Guide To The Understanding
 And Practice Of Spiritual Healing

James Redfield : The Celestine Prophecy

Printed in Great Britain
by Amazon